Diamond . . .
A Girl's Best Friend

Lessons Learned From My Dog

Rose M. Jarvis

xulon
PRESS

Copyright © 2010 by Rose M. Jarvis

Diamond . . . A Girl's Best Friend
by Rose M. Jarvis

Printed in the United States of America

ISBN 9781615798025

All rights reserved solely by the author. The author guarantees all contents are original and do not infringe upon the legal rights of any other person or work. No part of this book may be reproduced in any form without the permission of the author. The views expressed in this book are not necessarily those of the publisher.

Unless otherwise indicated, Bible quotations are taken from the Kings James Version of the Bible. Copyright © 2001 by G.E.M Publishing.

www.xulonpress.com

Dedication

This book is dedicated to:

Richard Jarvis
My husband, who has stood by me through everything; he is my partner and best friend.

LaToya S. Jarvis and Felicia R. Jarvis
My daughters, for all their help and support.

Nadine Greene and Regina Smith
For their prayers and support.

*James P. Carpenter
and Shirley A. Cosby Carpenter*

My parents, who have gone to be with the Lord, for all their years of encouragement, support, love and especially for their prayers.

Table of Contents

	Introduction	ix
Lesson 1	Diamond's Character	11
Lesson 2	Attitude	22
Lesson 3	Forgiveness	37
Lesson 4	When We Praise the Lord	46
Lesson 5	He Will Direct Our Paths	53
Lesson 6	Stormy Weather	61
Lesson 7	Jealousy	65
Lesson 8	Laugh Out Loud	71
Lesson 9	A New Owner	76
Lesson 10	The Life Line	83
Lesson 11	Endure Until the End	89
Lesson 12	High Praise	95

Diamond . . . A Girl's Best Friend

Lesson 13	Know Your Territory	102
Lesson 14	Lean On Him	113
Lesson 15	Unmovable Faith	122
Lesson 16	Change	130
Lesson 17	From the Pit to the Palace	136
Lesson 18	Be Real	142
Lesson 19	Be Still	148
Lesson 20	Another Way	158
Lesson 21	The First Kiss	166
Lesson 22	Awareness	171
	Conclusion	179

Introduction

My dog Diamond, a mix of a Rat Terrier and Pit Bull, was given to me several years ago by a friend. I didn't know it then, but what a blessing I received in bringing her home to live with me, my husband Ricky and my two daughters LaToya and Felicia. We learn from the word of God that He can use anyone or anything to teach us every day lessons. These lessons are so we can improve our own lives, and God has truly used my dog Diamond to help me grow to be a better person. When I've spoken to others about the lessons I have learned from Diamond they have asked me when would I put these lessons in writing. I'm thankful for the opportunity to have done that in this book.

When God opens your eyes with a better way to live life it should be shared with others. I pray that this book will be life changing for everyone that reads it. My prayer is that they will see them selves through the life examples of my dog Diamond and know that God wants to use Diamond to help them grow spiritually, mentally, and physically. This is truly my prayer for every reader.

Lesson 1

Diamond's Character

Diamond is a dog so she barks. When Diamond goes outside to use the bathroom she will come to the door and bark to let us know she is ready to come back inside. If someone knocks at the door, or rings the door bell Diamond will bark to let us know someone is there. Barking is what dogs do to communicate. I have never heard Diamond meow. She barks because she is a dog and that is how dogs speak. If someone would try to tell me they heard my dog meow, I would not believe them. I would not call the person a liar; I would simply think he or she must be mistaken. They must have heard a cat but saw Diamond. You can meow at Diamond all day and night but Diamond will only respond with a bark not a meow because it is not her character to meow.

   I was once accused of doing something I would never have done; it wasn't my character. If you're ever accused of something that you know you did not do, it will trouble your spirit. When you're being accused by someone you love, it not only troubles your spirit it also hurts. After I was accused, I had to take the matter to God in prayer. After telling God why it was hurting so much, and how I could not believe I was being accused of something that was not even my character, the Holy Spirit had me look at Diamond.

   'What does Diamond do that's a part of her character?" He asked.

   I responded, "She always barks."

   "Does Diamond ever meow?" the Spirit asked me.

Of course my answer was no, she never meows; it's not her character. It was as if a light bulb were turned on inside of me. The Holy Spirit will always lead, guide and direct you. What the Holy Spirit was saying to me was, no matter what, Diamond responds in her own character. When someone calls you out of your character your response should be in your character. My heart was no longer heavy, my spirit was renewed and my mind was made up.

This is when I thought about Jesus Himself on the cross. They had beaten Jesus so bad that if His own mother did not know it was Him, She would have not been able to identify her own son. If that was not enough they put thorns on His head, made Him carry His own cross and even spit in His face. In order to have Him crucified they even had people lie on Him. Jesus still went to the cross for them all. He could have called angels but He didn't. He could have come down off of the cross yet He stayed in the will of His Father. While Jesus was hanging on the cross after being beaten He cried out to God:

Father, forgive them, for they know not what they do – Luke 23:43

No matter what they said or did to Him, Jesus responded in His character. His response to everything his persecutors did to Him was a prayer on their behalf.

I know it does not feel good to be lied on, talked about, or used. However, if they did it to the only Son of God we know they will do it to us too. Jesus went through more then, than we will every go through in life. Yet, He did only what He knew the Father would have Him to do or say; He stayed in the will of His father. God is our heavenly father too and as His children we must stay in the father's will as Jesus did while He was here on earth. Do not waste your time trying to prove yourself; allow your true character to shine so brightly that the world will know that whatever you have been accused of could not be true. Stay in your character at all times. Do not allow anyone to cause you to come out of character. Your true character will speak for you without you even saying a word. We must learn how to say as Jesus said,

Father, forgive them; for they know not what they do. – Luke 23:43

Never allow people to cause you to do anything or say anything you would not normally do or say. If you do this you will be making it seem like they were right and you really did or said whatever you were accused of. If you allow the lie or anything else to cause you to be bound, you're not living in the liberty of the Lord. I know it doesn't feel good. I've been there but the truth sets us free!

Sometimes, it's not a false accusation; sometimes it may be your family, friends, spouse, or even your children wanting you to do something you do not want to do and because you will not do it they all turn against you. Never allow anyone to have control of you but God. Jesus has set us free and in the word of God Jesus said:

If the Son sets you free, you will be free in deed – John 8:36

We should never allow ourselves to be under the yoke of bondage again. Galatians 5:1 says:

It is for freedom that Christ has set us free. Stand firm, then, and do not let yourselves be burdened again by a yoke of slavery.

He paid the highest price which could be paid to set you free so stay free; live in the peace that passes all understanding.

Let's say for instance, you feel lead to attend a different church apart from your family. Every church is not for everyone. You know what it takes to feed your spirit and what it needs so why would you stay in a church where you're not getting fed spiritually just to be with your family? You would be dying spiritually, and that is a form of bondage. Once you find the right church you will know it is the right church for you because your spirit will let you know you're home. Then, when you follow that leading, you're looked at as a cast away, but why live in bondage when you can be free?

When my husband and I leave the house, we close the bedroom doors so that Diamond will not jump onto the beds, and we cover our furniture. Her bed is placed in the hallway upstairs so that she can lay down when she wants too. Now Diamond will not get on the furniture while we're at home but when we leave she jumps right up on the beds or couch if we don't do this before we go. Even with the couch covered, Diamond is so smart that she will wait until we leave then somehow remove just enough of the covering from the couch to lie against a pillow. To stop her, we had to start putting items on top of the covers so that there was no room for her to get up on the couch at all.

When we come home, I open the bedroom doors allowing Diamond to run around the house more freely. All I have to say is "Okay Diamond, you can move around more now," and she will take off like someone is chasing her. It's so amusing that I just stand there and watch to see how many times she will run back and forth. Diamond runs so fast you cannot even see her back feet touch the floor, and she continues until my husband gets tired of hearing her running back and forth. When Diamond hears him yell her name she stops and goes to get something to drink. I'm sure she does not like being left in the hallway everyday while we go to work, and when the doors are reopened Diamond freely expresses how excited she is about her freedom to access every room in the house.

Live in the spirit of freedom. When you're not allowed to be yourself then the "true you" that God created will never be seen on earth. If the true you is never seen, then you will never fulfill your purpose in life. God created you to do something that no one else has been created to do. When you stand before

Him you cannot say what you did not do because no one believed in you. God is not going to want to hear that; you cannot use others as an excuse to why you did not do what you were created to fulfill. The sky is the limit so shake off what they said. Shake off what they did, pray for them and go on with your life.

Some people will only remember you according to what you use to do or what you use to say; that's the old you. I love the story in I Kings 3:16-27. There is a story about two harlots that came to King Solomon. Both of them had babies but one of them lay on her child during the night and killed the baby then exchanged her deceased infant for the living baby. The other mother knew the deceased child was not her baby yet she had to prove it to get her baby back. She goes before the king hoping he will not judge her according to her past but that he would see the change she has made and allow her to take her baby home. The baby had changed her. It was no longer all about what she wanted or what she needed. Now that she was blessed by

God with the gift of life she had changed. She was blessed with a son and she wanted to take care of the child. The other harlot turned back and in her turning she killed her son. She was still selfish and still only caring about her own interests and no one else's. She takes the baby away from her roommate and places her dead baby in the bed of her roommate. She never mourns for her son, nor does she show any sorrow. When they both tell the king that the living baby is her own, the king tells the guide to bring a sword (word) and cut the baby in half, then give one half to one mother and the other half to the other mother. The real mother speaks up showing her new character:

> *O my lord, give her the living child, and in no wise slay it, but the other said, Let it be neither mine nor yours, but divide it – I Kings 3:26*

The true mother had changed and her new character was truly seen by the king. She was no longer the same and the king could tell it. The woman walked in her character and was blessed to get her baby back. He knew she was the real mother and he gave the baby to her for he could see the other women had not changed and was still selfish, only wanting what was best for her.

Now while the mother had changed, she failed to change her company. When we change our lives we must also change our company. If the people we use to hang with do not make the same change, we have to leave them alone. We will continue to pray that they will give their life to God as we have but we cannot force them to do so. Make sure you go all the way with your new life in Christ Jesus. You're a new creature in Christ. Your past needs to stay in the past.

Lesson 2

Attitude

Diamond greets me at the door everyday with exhortation. Even when Diamond has been left at home alone for hours she never changes her attitude. Sometimes I've come home and there is no food or water in her bowl (the children had forgotten to fill it before they left) and although she may be hungry, she is still happy to see Ricky and me come home. Diamond greets her master with the attitude of praise no matter what kind of day she has had. When I see Diamond's appreciation towards me the same response echoes back to her.

Your attitude shows the way you allow things to affect you whether positive or negative. We echo what is really in our hearts through the way we respond. The word of God tells us:

Be steadfast, immovable, always abounding in the work of the Lord, knowing that your labor is not in vain in the Lord. – I Corinthians 15:58

Your attitude is your frame of mind. If you want to have a good day echo positive words; start the day with the right attitude. Do not allow everyday issues to dictate how your day will turn out. We're to rejoice in the Lord always, meaning for eternity! Everyday of your life can be overflowing with triumph when you faithfully trust God.

The Shunammite woman in II Kings is a good example for us to focus our attention on to help develop an attitude of gratitude. The Bible calls her a notable woman (II Kings 4:8). She noticed that the man of God, Elisha and his servant, Gehazi would pass by her house regularly (II Kings 4:9) and persuaded him to eat food at her house whenever he would pass by. She did not want anything from him; this woman was just so grateful to be able to serve the man of God. Because she did it for the right reason she was able to do it with the right attitude. Knowing that Elisha was doing the Lord's will, this woman used wisdom when talking to her husband concerning him. She was able to convince her husband that they should do more than just feed the man of God. They added an upper room to their home so whenever Elisha passed by he could not only eat but also rest from his journey (II Kings 4:9-11). Although the woman is not looking for anything in return, the man of God calls her and tells her she will have a son the following year (II Kings 4:16). The woman's husband was old and they had no children. II Kings 4:17 says she conceived and bore a son just as the man of God had said would happen at the appointed time.

The Shunammite woman's son grew but one day while his father was working the young boy complained about his head hurting him. The boy's father had one of the workers take him to his mother. After lying on his mother's lap until noon, the young boy died. I love the attitude of this woman. She does not complain, she just picks her son up and places his body on Elisha's bed in the upper room. There is no crying or questioning God, just wisdom, faith and hope in action. After placing his body on the bed she calls for her husband to send a servant with a donkey so she can go see the man of God and come back (II Kings 4:22). When her husband questions her going to see the man of God, she replies, "It shall be well" (II Kings 4:23). What an attitude of faith in God and His servant. We too must learn to live in faith for without faith we cannot please God (Hebrews 11:6). When the servant comes to take her to the man of God she tells him to ride with no slack for her unless she instructs him differently during the journey. What I see here is even with her loss she expects no mercy from man. This is so powerful because too often we want the whole world to focus around our pain and circumstances instead of walking in victory. When Elisha sees the woman coming he sends Gehazi to meet her and ask her three questions (II Kings 4:26).

The first question was, "Is everything well with you?"

The Shunammite woman replies, "It is well."

Second question: "Is it well with your husband?"

She replies again, "It is well."

His last question: "Is it well with the child?"

The woman replies, "It is well."

Although the Shunammite woman's soul was vexed and troubled within her, she never spoke death with her mouth; she moved in faith. Look at her attitude. Can you feel her faith in action? Can you see the trust in God and in his servant Elisha? The boy is at home dead on Elisha's bed, yet she speaks in faith. The Bible teaches us:

Death and life are in the power of the tongue; and they that love it shall eat the fruit thereof
– Proverbs 18:21

What kind of fruit have you been eating lately? Have you been killing all of your fruit from the root with your words? We all will be faced with many different things in life but my question to you is what have you called it? What have you named the issue? Did you ever stop to think about the reality of your words? If you're always saying, 'things will never change' then guess what - they will not change because you have been naming it and claiming it to be the same.

Negative words attract negativity, positive words attract positivity. It's almost like a magnet. When you come into the presence of a positive person, their positive attitude causes you to shift gears. You could have come in down and out but just by being in that individual's presence everything shifts to line up with the flow of the magnetic force that's pulling you into motion. On the other hand you may come into the presence of someone who is always negative. Before you came into their presence you were feeling fine with no worries or cares but the magnetic pull coming from them shifts you and now you do not know what's wrong with you; all of a sudden you're down. We have to make sure we continue to speak health, life and faith while in that negative person's presence. We cannot allow them to shift our gears. You speak life and cause the negative person to be drawn by your source of positivity. If you allow them to draw you then you come into agreement with them, which will cause you to become negative too.

I heard a true story about a man that did an experiment with rice. He put the same kind of white rice, in the same amounts into two identical jars with identical lids on each. He placed them in the same room under the same conditions. The only difference was that he labeled each jar with a piece of paper reading different words. One jar was labeled with the words, "I love you and I hope you live forever" and the other was labeled with the words "I hate you and I hope you die soon." After 81 days he saw that the contents of the two jars were no longer the same. The jar that had been labeled with the loving sentiments could still be identified as white rice. The jar that had been negatively labeled no longer looked like rice. The rice had turned black, its shape changed into round balls, and mold had begun to grow inside the jar. Now rice cannot see, think, smell or talk. Yet, the power of the words that the jars had been labeled with caused the rice to do exactly what was written about it. How much more stronger do you think our actions work in our lives? Fall in love with yourself. Look in the mirror and tell yourself that your father loves you. He loves you so much that He made you in His image and likeness. You're somebody because God does not make junk. Get up from that bed of hurt, fear, worry and confusion. Fix yourself up but do not do it for anyone else; do it for yourself! You have to learn how to love you! Build up your confidence by speaking positive about everything. Stay focused, stay positive, and most of all stay in faith.

When the Shunammite woman got to the man of God, she caught him by his feet. I find this very interesting too because the word of God in Ephesians

6:15 talks about the feet being shod with the preparation of the gospel of peace. She holds on to his peace which helps her keep her peace. When she is able to speak to the man of God she still does not call her situation dead! She addresses him with questions causing him to remember her words she had spoken when he gave her the word of promise for the son. Elisha sends Gehazi to the woman's house with instructions on what to do once he got there. The mother of the child tells Elisha in faith,

As the Lord lives: and as your soul lives I will not leave you – II Kings 4:30

What faith she has in the man of God. She said to her husband in the 22nd verse that she would run to the man of God and come back. Here she tells Elisha that she will not leave him as long as he lives and as long as the Lord lives! She speaks in faith knowing he will not send her back alone but would come with her to see about the gift God had given

Diamond . . . A Girl's Best Friend

her and her husband.

Gehazi goes ahead of them and does what Elisha had instructed him to do with the child. Before Elisha and the woman make it back to the house, Gehazi meets them and tells Elisha that the child did not respond. The Shunammite woman is still holding on to her peace; she stays focused. Notice that Elisha doesn't have to say anything to her along the way, not even after she heard the report coming from Gehazi. When Elisha gets to the house he does not allow the woman or Gehazi to come into the room with him. He goes in, shuts the door and prays to God. After laying on the child the Bible says he returned in the house and walked back and forth before returning to the child. Now maybe you did not catch it; Elisha left the room where the child lay and went where the servant and the mother of the child were waiting and walks back and forth. Can you imagine how the enemy could have tried to mess with her mind? The word of God says:

The weapons of our warfare are not carnal, but mighty through God to the pulling down of strong holds: casting down imaginations; and every high thing that exalts itself against the knowledge of God; and bringing into captivity every thought to the obedience of Christ – II Corinthians 10:4-5

Notice it is up to us to cast it down not God! He is giving us the power to pull down every strong hold. Somethings we do not need to pray about; we just need to operate in the authority God has given us dominion to walk in.

Elisha went back up to the room again (he did not give up nor did he give in) and this time the child sneezed seven times, and then opened his eyes. Elisha sent for Gehazi to have him call the mother. When she comes into the room Elisha tells her to pick up her son (II Kings 4:36). She comes in, falls at Elisha's feet and bows to the ground. Before she takes up her son she worships. This time she is not holding on to his feet. This time she releases her peace in the form of worship. This woman served the Lord's servant with the right attitude. Have you ever seen someone serving in the house of the Lord at the door ushering the people in with a nasty spirit? You come in and say good morning and they ask you what's so good about it? She serves with the right attitude and with no hidden motives.

Elisha leaves and goes to Gilgal. Chapters later God called a famine (II Kings 8:1) that would last seven years. Elisha spoke to the woman and told her about the famine on the way, instructing her to take her family and go where she could for the seven years. She does not complain. She does what the man of God instructs her to do and leaves her home. After the seven years were over the woman goes back and goes before the king to appeal for her house and land. When she comes before the king Gehazi is there telling him about the great things God worked through the man of God. As Gehazi tells the king about the woman's son that Elisha brought back to life, the woman walks in with her son. The king asked the woman to tell him about what Gehazi had just told him. She confirms the words. When she finished testifying about the goodness of the Lord it caused the king to do something for her and her family. II Kings 8:6 tells us the king appointed a certain officer for her, saying:

Restore all that was hers and all the proceeds of the field from the day that she left the land until now.

Look at the hand of God moving on behalf of His own. She and her family did not lose anything. Everything was restored to the family. Even the proceeds that came in while they were gone. As children of God we do not need to worry; God takes care of His own.

Sometimes in the night Diamond has to go to the bathroom. Everyone is home but she will not go to anyone else but me. I can be sound asleep but she will jump up on the side of my bed to wake me up. She knows not to wake my husband because she knows he will not get up with her nor will he walk her outside. The children love her just as much as I do but Diamond knows they're not going to get up and walk her in the middle of the night. Diamond knows her master will not only get up but will also walk her then give her something to eat if she wants it. She knows that I will take good care of her and I won't ignore her when she needs me.

You should always go to the one that will love you unconditionally. Go to God for He knows what's best for you. Never decide anything without asking God for direction. When you allow Him to lead the way you cannot go wrong. He has promised never to leave us nor forsake us in our time of need. In the presence of the Lord there is fullness of joy so stay in his presence! Jesus has a way of giving you a peace that passes all understanding. Allow Him not only to be your Savior, permit Him to be your Lord. Commit yourself to the Lordship of Jesus Christ and he will echo back to you blessings of favor spiritually, economically and socially when you really trust Him. Change your negative attitude to one that God will get glory from. You are the light of the world, the salt of the earth and a new creation in Christ Jesus. Do not allow a Diamond to out shine a child of God. The Holy Spirit is inside of you waiting to help you through every storm that comes your way. Allow Him to lead guide and direct your life which will cause you to live a life of praise.

Lesson 3

Forgiveness

Whenever Diamond has an accident in the house, she will always go to the same spot in our dining room. Normally, when I get home she will come running to me glad to see me but on any day that she's had an accident, she will not come to me. When she does not greet me at the door, I will yell her name, knowing what must have happened while we were away. Instead of coming she will avoid me and hide. After cleaning up the mess, I'm mad for a little while but then I will call her and let her know I am not mad anymore. She will slowly come over to me, and once I begin to pet her, she receives the love and then goes about the day as if nothing ever happened. Once she knows I'm over it she does not allow it to stop her from coming to me for anything she needs.

I John 1:9 says:

If we confess our sins, He is faithful and just to forgive us of all our sins and to cleanse us from all unrighteousness.

Even though we know what the word says we allow the enemy to cause us to lose sleep over our past. Whatever you have done, if you have repented sincerely from your heart, it's as if you never did it. The Bible says:

As far as the east is from the west, so far has He removed our transgressions from us – Psalm 103:12

Jesus came that we might have life and have it more abundantly. If you're not free from your past, you're not experiencing his abundant joy. Start today. Receive His love, grace, and mercy right now. Repent sincerely from your heart, then allow the comfort of the Holy Spirit to assure you that your "accidents" have been covered under the blood of Jesus Christ. Be set free and release that heavy weight so you can start enjoying life.

In Luke chapter 15, we find the story of the Prodigal Son. This young man asked his father to give him his share of wealth while his father was still living. He should not have received it until the father died, yet he wanted it while his father still lived. The father gave him his share of wealth, and with it the young man went into a far country. There he wasted his substance with riotous living. After he had spent all of his money, a mighty famine arose in that land and he began to be in want. He ended up in the field feeding swine. No one would give him anything to eat. He would have filled his belly with the husks that the swine did eat but he came to himself. While he had money, he had many friends; many of them helped him spend the money, but when it was all gone they went too. Real friends will be there when you do not have and are in need, not only when you have. He goes back home humble enough to be willing to work as a servant for his father. He knows he has sinned against heaven and against his father. The Bible says the father saw him coming while he was still afar off and had compassion. The father ran to him, fell on his neck and kissed him. He has the servants put a robe, a ring and shoes on his son. Then he ordered them to kill the fat calf and calls for a celebration. The father proclaimed,

For this my son was dead, and is alive again; he was lost, and is found. – Luke 15:24

The father never gave up on his son; God never wants to give up on us either. We all fall short of the glory of God but He waits for us to repent and get back in order. There are many actions and decisions I have personally made in my life that I regret. Now that I'm older, I wonder what in the world was I ever thinking about when I did what I did in my past. You cannot change what you did but you can be forgiven for it. Why carry it around when God's grace is for everyone that is willing to accept it by just repenting sincerely from your heart to God? Psalm 32:5 says,

> *I acknowledged my sin to you and did not cover up my iniquity. I said, "I will confess my transgressions to the Lord" and you forgave the guilt of my sin.*

God will forgive you when you sincerely repent. The question then is, can you forgive yourself? I meet so many people that think just because they have made mistakes since they have given their lives to the Lord that God doesn't still love them. He loves and cares for you very much. When you fall short, go to Him in prayer and ask for His forgiveness. You're His child now and His "love is as strong as death" (Song of Solomon 8:6). You can't change what you did but you can learn from it and go on to live under the grace of our Lord teaching others about His amazing grace. I love everyone; people often ask me why I'm always trying to help everyone. All I can say is when God saved me He really did change me to think about others more then myself. I believe all of God's children should be that way and care more about others. Show and share the love of God so that the Kingdom of God will be enlarged.

God wants you to experience His mercy and grace so you can help someone else find it too. There is an old saying, "live and learn." As we live from day to day we learn from our mistakes and grow from them to become better people. What the Prodigal Son did was wrong, yet his earthly father was still looking for him to come back home. God is willing and able to do more for us than what our earthly father can ever do for us. How many marriages would be better if spouses just learned to forgive each other? When

God makes us one in marriage we're really just mad with ourselves when we get mad with our spouse because we're one. Too many people say they love God, and they're His children but how can we say we love Him when we do not even love the ones we have around us on a daily basis? That's something to think about.

Children can teach us adults a thing or two if we will allow them. If you've ever watched children when they play, you will notice that if they get mad with one another, it lasts only for a little while. Within a few minutes you will see them playing together like nothing ever happened. Adults will take anger and grudges to their graves before they will forgive one another. I remember a friend telling me that her father and Aunt did not get along as brother and sister. Since they did not get along the aunt looked down on her brother's children. The brother died but the Aunt still treated the children with disdain because of the negative relationship she and her brother shared. Her brother's children even go to the same church but that has not softened the aunt's heart.

How can we say we love God when we cannot love our brothers and sisters in Christ? Jesus forgave us for all our sins. God loved us so much that He sent His only Son to die for us and we can't even forgive those who wronged us here on earth after we have been forgiven. Jesus said:

But I say to you, love your enemies, bless them that curse you, do good to them that hate you, and pray for them which spitefully use you, and persecute you – Matthew 5:44

Wait a minute, not only do we have to forgive them; but Jesus tells us to love them too, not just our friends that did us wrong - but even our enemies! Love, bless, do good to them and pray for them!

It sounds like Jesus wants all of us to follow in His foot steps. He would not tell us to do something that we could not do. I know you're saying *but you do not know what they did to me.* I may not know, but God knows. It may seem like they will be getting away with what ever it was they did to you, but they will reap what they've sowed; you just need to be free from it. Now if Jesus tells us to do all of this for our enemies, surely He wants you to forgive yourself. Get over it so that it will not control you and stop you from enjoying your life. The price has been paid for you to be free so walk in the freeness of Christ. Live each day as if it's your last day; start living life to the fullest. Tell the devil, "I will live and not die; I will declare the work of my Lord while I yet live." He paid the price for you to be free so accept it today.

Lesson 4

When We Praise the Lord

I was admitted into the hospital for two weeks so my oldest daughter, LaToya, kept Diamond at her house for me. When I was released to come home, I was not yet able to take care of Diamond myself, so LaToya kept her another two weeks. During that time, she came to visit and brought Diamond with her. At that point, it had been about three and a half weeks since Diamond had seen me. She was so happy to see me that she jumped up as high as five feet to kiss me about 20 times in a row!

Diamond . . . A Girl's Best Friend

The children and my sister laughed at Diamond's excitement yet that didn't stop her from leaping for joy. She was so happy to be in my presence again she did not allow them to stop her from expressing her love towards me. Diamond did not wait for me to give her anything before she decided to express her love; she just showered me with love as soon as she came into my bedroom.

Too often we allow others to stop us from giving God praise when we come into His house. No one in the house of God has done more for you than what the Lord has done for you. No one should be able to stop you from worshiping Him in His sanctuary. When Mary was carrying baby Jesus she went to visit her cousin Elizabeth after being told by the angel that Elizabeth was also pregnant (Luke 1:36). When Mary got to Elizabeth and greeted her, the baby in Elizabeth's womb began to leap for joy. Here you have a baby that is still in the development stages giving God more praise than some of us that have been born and are already filled with the Holy Spirit. Jesus had not yet been born but baby John still gave Him praise. Jesus had not yet gone to the cross for us, yet John was able to leap for joy just being in His presence. John was in a dark place yet he did not allow his surroundings to stop his praise. If we would just begin to praise the Lord maybe we would be filled with what we need to make it in life.

Can you praise God while you're still in your dark place? Can you believe God can bring you out of your dark place? If you will just begin to praise Him right now in spite of what's going on, He will come to your rescue. The Bible tells us how we're to seek first the Kingdom of God then everything else will be added, but many times we wait until something is added before we decide to praise God. Many battles were won in the Bible just from the people praising God. They did not have to fight! Their praise caused God to fight for them. When you really begin to leap for joy in the presence of God anything that's attached to you that should not

Diamond . . . A Girl's Best Friend

be will begin to drop off. Praise is very powerful and the enemy knows this; that's why he tries to stop you from doing it.

If you're in a church that will not allow you to praise God, that church is going against what the word of God teaches us to do every time we enter into the house of the Lord. When you begin to praise God, you want to forget about everyone around you like Diamond did. She did not allow those around her to stop her from leaping up and kissing me over and over again.

Diamond also ran right to me. When you go to church get as close to the front as you can; there are many distractions in the back of the sanctuary. When you come in, put all your worries down and focus on worshiping God. When you lift your hands, it's a sign off surrendering unto the Lord. Lift your hands, close your eyes, open your mouth and begin to worship the Lord with thanksgiving. Do not ask Him for anything, just think about His faithfulness unto you and thank Him for everything while the blood is still running warm in your veins. Give God a crazy praise!

I think we forget how blessed we are just to be able to get up in the morning and dress ourselves. While I was in the hospital, just taking a bath would take me at least an hour and a half. I was in so much pain and doing anything the first two weeks took a lot of energy and strength. My doctor told me that walking would help the healing process so I walked at least three times a day. As I walked the halls of the hospital I saw many people in rooms who weren't able to walk or do anything for themselves. I began to praise God for allowing me to walk and take care of myself again.

One lady was sitting in the waiting area for her loved one's doctor to come back in with the report from an operation. She told me that her sister-in-law had the same operation that I'd had but her condition had been cancerous yet mine was not. You can be going through something and someone else is going through the same thing but under worse circumstances. Instead of focusing on our needs and our wants, we should show our love for God by helping someone else. Although I was not completely healed when I talked to the lady in the waiting room, I stopped and had prayer with her for her sister-in-law. God wants us to continue to praise Him by helping someone else while we wait for Him to move on our behalf.

After I left her, I began to praise God even more. We should never complain if we really trust God to be able to bring us out of whatever we're in. We must remember if it's something that God wants us to learn we will remain in it until we complete the lesson. Many times we just need to let go and let God have His way. If it's something that you just have not walked in dominion in for yourself then you will not be able to change the situation until you take authority over it. God has given you the power and a measure of faith to be able to handle it; He is not going to do anything for you that he has given you the authority to fix yourself.

Diamond knew I was still not completely healed; she would come to the bedside and just check on me. She did not try to get me to do things that I would normally do with her, she just kept checking on me and giving me kisses every time she could reach me.

When was the last time you just went into the presence of God just to see Him - not looking for anything or asking for anything, just kissing your heavenly father with love from your heart?

Lesson 5

He Will Direct Our Paths

While walking Diamond sometimes she will try to go in a ditch or in the woods. I will pull her back because in the ditch there is dirty water which could be covering snakes. In the woods there can be thorns that can get on her and hurt her. She cannot see the danger but as her master I protect her by pulling her away from the wrong path. God does the same thing for us.

Proverbs 3:5-6 says:

Trust in the Lord with all your heart, and lean not on your own understanding, in all your ways acknowledge Him, and He shall direct your paths.

The Holy Spirit will lead, guide, and direct us in all our ways. Sometimes we can't see danger or we think a thing is good for us but God knows best. He will pull us back and direct us in the way we should take.

In Acts, there is a story about a young man name Saul who was on the wrong path of destroying God's church, and badly needed direction. Saul was so lost that he believed that his actions of wreaking havoc on the church were actually right, and gave it his all. He tore into people's homes to arrest not just men but women also, placing them into prison just for being Christians. The people of the church were all scattered abroad throughout the regions of Judaea and Samaria, except for the apostles. Saul had even gone to the high priest and requested letters to Damascus to the synagogues, granting him permission to arrest, bind and bring any followers of the Lord Jesus Christ bound to Jerusalem where there was great persecution against the church.

As he journeyed to Damascus seeking more Christians to persecute, a bright light shined down on him from heaven causing him to fall to the earth. He heard a voice call him by name twice. Not only did the voice call him, but it also asked him a question:

Saul, Saul, why persecute you Me? – Acts 22:7

Even though Saul did not know who the voice belonged to, or where it came from, in his response he called him Lord. Jesus tells Saul it is He whom he has been persecuting. Saul is now trembling and astonished; he knows this power must be the real thing. The men that journeyed with Saul stood speechless, hearing the voice, but seeing no man.

Saul asks Jesus what He would have him to do for Him. Jesus gives Saul instructions; when Saul gets up from the ground he opens his eyes but cannot see. The men that were with him led him by the hand and brought him into Damascus. Saul was three days without sight, neither did he eat or drink. Unbeknownst to Saul, The Lord had chosen him to bear His name before the Gentiles, kings, and the children of Israel. Saul not only needed his eye sight back, he also needed to be filled with the Holy Spirit.

There was a disciple by the name of Ananias at Damascus. The Lord spoke to him and told him to go into the street which was called Straight, and to inquire in the house of Judas for Saul. Saul had done so much evil that everyone had heard about him. Ananias reminds the Lord about the evil Saul had done to the saints in Jerusalem, but God sent Ananias to pray for Saul and to lay hands on him so that he would be filled with the Holy Spirit.

What I like about this story is Saul is so lost,

Diamond . . . A Girl's Best Friend

he had to be guided to a house on a street called Straight. Straight would place him on the road leading to new direction for his life. Saul's life was totally turned around for the better and the Lord changed his name from Saul to Paul. He trusted God's guidance. I'm not saying his life was full of roses thereafter; it was far from it. Many Christians did not trust him for they knew all the wrong he did while on the wrong path. He had to be let down out of a window in a basket to get away from people that wanted to kill him. He was beaten and left for dead, and went to prison many times. (He wrote most of the Bible while he was in prison.) He was bitten by a poisonous snake and even shipwrecked but still he stayed focused and trusted the guidance of the Holy Spirit. Once he allowed the Lord Jesus to be head of his life, no matter what happened, he knew he was never alone.

Before he was killed he says powerful words to the young preacher Timothy in the Epistle:

For I am now ready to be offered, and the time of my departure is at hand. I have fought a good fight, I have finished my course, I have kept the faith: Hereafter there is laid up for me a crown of righteousness, which the Lord, the righteous judge, shall give me at that day: and not to me only, but to all them also that love His appearing.
– II Timothy 4:6-8

Many people gave their lives to the Lord because of the preaching and teaching Paul did all over the world for the Lord. He got on the right path plus he helped many others find the right path too. Have you ever been lost in a car trying to figure out how to get somewhere? You stop and ask someone how to get to your destination but they get you more lost then you were before. Now, we have this item called a navigation system, or GPS as they are most frequently called, that will get you to where you need to go once you put in your location and desired destination. The GPS will tell you when to turn and when to stay straight; it will even tell you how much time and distance you have left to go before you get to your destination. If you miss your turn and start going the wrong way the GPS will get you back on track. God is our spiritual GPS when we need direction for anything in life He tells us to come to Him. Even if we just need rest, Jesus wants our path to lead directly to Him that is able to give us rest:

Jesus said, come to me, all you who are weary and burdened, and I will give you rest. – Matthew 11:28

Does your life need direction right about now? There is a road called Straight just for you; ask God to lead you to it. Have you lost your job? Ask God to help you find another one. Not only will He help you find another job but it will be a better job waiting just for you if you allow Him to direct your paths. Has the Lord placed a dream in your spirit that you want to fulfill? Allow Him to give you the wisdom needed to bring the dream to pass. There is nothing too hard for God. There is no problem he cannot solve. Give it to Him and let Him map out the way to success for you. He offers His help free of charge.

Lesson 6

Stormy Weather

Whenever it storms, Diamond will tremble in fear until she can get to me. She knows when she gets to me I will allow her to sit on my lap. After she gets in my lap she will wag her tail. The storm is still going on but because she is now in my lap she knows she's safe.

When Peter and the other disciples were in a boat in the midst of a storm, and Jesus walked out to meet them, I find it interesting to read that Peter did not ask Jesus to stop the storm. Peter just asked

Him if he could come to Him. When Jesus gave him permission, Peter got out of the boat and walked toward Jesus. As Peter was going to Jesus he saw the strong winds and became afraid and began to sink. He cried out to the Lord to save him and Jesus stretched out His hand and caught him. Peter was saved by the Lord yet he still never asked the Lord to stop the storm. The Bible says:

When they were come into the ship, the wind ceased. – Matthew 14:32

When the Lord is on board with you it does not matter if it's storming around you; you will not sink.

Luke 8:23 tells another story about a storm that took place while they were in a ship together going to the other side as Jesus had told them. A storm of wind came down on the lake while Jesus was asleep on the boat. Jesus was able to sleep in peace during a storm because he trusted his father (Matthew

8:23-26). We must trust our heavenly father; surely he can handle our storms. The Bible says:

But let all those rejoice who put their trust in You: let them ever shout for joy, because You defend them: let those also who love Your name be joyful in You. For You, O Lord, will bless the righteous; with favor You will surround him as with a shield.
— Psalm 5:11-12

If Jesus is resting in the midst of a storm and He has promised to protect us when we're in a storm then we need to just go to Him and rest with Him in faith.

In a strong Tropical storm the eye wall is a ring of towering thunderstorms where the most severe weather occurs. The eye of a storm is at the center of the storm, yet the eye is a region of mostly calm weather even though it is surrounded by severe weather. In all storms the eye is the location of the storm's minimum pressure. This is so powerful because the eye wall surrounds the eye but the eye stays calm. The issue you face may be surrounding you, yet you can stay calm right in the eye of the storm in your life.

Lesson 7

Jealousy

My oldest daughter LaToya has a little boy named Daveon, and my youngest daughter Felicia has a daughter named Emani. Whenever the babies came to visit us at home, we made sure Diamond was not jealous of them. I've heard some terrible stories about dogs killing babies, jealous of the love their owners would show them. Diamond did just the opposite thing with my grandchildren; she became their protector.

Whenever someone would come to the house to congratulate the girls and to see the babies, Diamond would not let them near the cribs. She would crawl and stand ready to attack. The Pit Bull in her scares people that do not know her well, so as our friends and loved ones would come to see the babies we would have to move Diamond.

Diamond understood that we still loved her, yet we had more love to share with others too. She was not jealous at all, and now that the children are older they are able to run around and play with her and Diamond loves when they come to visit.

Jealousy and envy are two characteristics that are totally opposite of the way God tells us we should be with one another. He gave us what is called The Great Commandment:

Jesus said to him, you shall love the Lord your God with all your heart, and with all your soul, and with all your mind. – Matthew 22:37-39

This is the first and great (important) commandment.

And the second is like it,

You shall love your neighbor as yourself
– Matthew 19:19

Jesus says love your neighbor as yourself. If you do not love yourself then you cannot love your neighbor right. Who is your neighbor? Anyone you come in contact with becomes your neighbor. Many people do not love themselves and this is why they envy others and try to be like someone else. If you're not being yourself, then you're not being what God created. Be yourself; do not envy anyone for you do not know what they had to go through to get to where they may be.

I can remember when I first moved to Virginia from Long Island; I felt that the people in the south were not nice. You see, I grew up in a small place called Greenport, where we had only one traffic light in town and everyone knew each other and greeted each other. A car wasn't necessary; you could walk to the stores or wherever you needed to go. When I moved to Virginia, I brought my small town cordiality with me and would speak to the people that I came across, but they would look at me like I was crazy. One man asked me if I knew him; my response was,

"No sir, but do I have to know you personally to say hello?"

He said, "Young lady, you're very right; have a nice day."

I realized then that people weren't unfriendly; they just were not use to someone speaking to them if they did not know them.

In I Samuel chapter one there is a story about Elkanah and his two wives. His first wife's name was Hannah and the name of the other was Peninnah. Hannah had no children by her husband but he still loved her and he would give her double portions. Peninnah had children by her husband, yet, she was jealous of the love Elkanah showed to Hannah. Peninnah would provoke Hannah so much that she caused her to be bitter and tremble, thus making her

Diamond . . . A Girl's Best Friend

irritable because Jehovah had shut up her womb. Hannah went on a fast. Then she went into the temple to pray unto the Lord. She asked the Lord for a man child, promising to give him back unto the Lord. The priest Eli told her:

Go in peace and the God of Israel grant you your petition that you have asked of Him.
– I Samuel 1:17

When she left the temple she ended her fast and her countenance was no longer sad. She knew God had heard her prayer plus the man of God stood in agreement with her prayer request. Her family got up early the next morning and worshiped before the Lord before they returned to Ramah. When they returned home, Elkanah made love to his wife Hannah and the Lord opened her womb. Hannah conceived and bore Elkanah a son whom they named Samuel. After he was weaned she dedicated him to the Lord as long as he lived then prayed, rejoicing in the Lord.

Her womb had been opened, bringing Peninnah's provoking to an end.

Peninnah's jealousy caused Hannah to do something about her situation. What was intended for evil ended up being the very thing that hard-pressed Hannah into doing something about her adversary. She did not respond with an eye for an eye but instead Hannah reached out to God for help to handle the struggle within. Never allow the childish actions of your haters to cause you to become childish yourself. There is an appointed time for all of us, for God has no respect of persons (Romans 2:11). Knowing this, we should be happy when our brothers and sisters in the Lord are blessed. When friends and loved ones are blessed there should not be any jealousy, envy, negativity or anything like that seen in our attitude.

Lesson 8

Laugh Out Loud

*D*iamond *is very good at making me laugh. Whenever I take a bath, she will peek in the bathroom but will not come in because she thinks I'm going to give her a bath too and she hates taking baths. I can have a treat for her in my hand but because I'm in the bathroom she will not come to get it. After I finish my bath I put lotion on my body, including my feet and toes. Diamond loves the smell and taste of the products I use on my feet. If I do not put on slippers, Diamond will come over to me and lick my feet. I try to take her licking as long as*

I can without moving but it tickles so much I can't stop laughing. I'll tell her to stop and then move my feet, and she is obedient until she sees that I have stopped laughing. She will try to get to my feet and make me laugh again. The Bible tells us that laughter is good medicine. It's almost as if she knows the word of God.

When was the last time you had a good laugh? I have another question for you; when was the last time you made someone else laugh?

We are all troubled on every side, yet not distressed; we are perplexed, but not in despair; persecuted, but not forsaken; cast down, but not destroyed —II Corinthians 4:8-9

We faint not for we're renewed day by day by the power of our loving father. Psalm 37:1 says,

Fret not yourself because of evildoers, neither

be you envious against the workers of iniquity

In verse 13 of the same Psalm it tells us that the Lord laughs at them (the wicked ones). If the Lord laughs at them then why should you fret over them? Stop allowing them to steal your joy. Learn to laugh out loud. Maybe it's not someone but something like your bills that you need to laugh at. Put them all in the center of the floor and just laugh at them! Yes, you heard me right; laugh at them. When you do not allow them to sweat you then they're not over you! They too will pass away. Take them one by one and begin to speak to them. Call them all paid off in full in Jesus name.

If you love life and live it to the fullest, nothing can stop you from achieving. I remember an old song that simply said, "Don't worry be happy" and just from hearing that song people's negativity would shift positively. The sound of rain or water running has a way of helping you to relax. When you're laughing, you're not worrying. When you're laughing, you do not have time for doubting. When I was sick with cancer I told no one but God. I went to the Lord in prayer thanking Him that by His Son's stripes I would be healed. I knew I could not worry nor allow myself to be sad. I would go to movies and that would make me laugh. I would read His word and meditate on all His promises concerning healing. When I went to bed, I rested in Him for He said I could come to Him when I needed too. He has no respect of persons. What this means to you and I is that if He did it for one He will do it for you too. You can come to Him too.

What amazed me was that as I read all the stories in the Bible where He healed someone or someone walked in faith and received their healing, each story would cause me to smile! As I read them, not only was I smiling but my faith was being increased. Instead of worrying I was rejoicing over His trust in me to walk in faith with the issue of cancer. When I went back to the doctor two weeks later, there was not even a sign of what they had initially seen! God is so good and His mercy endures forever.

Diamond . . . A Girl's Best Friend

When I'm playing with Diamond I will take her toy from her then she will try to get it back from me. Diamond will jump up until she can reach it then she pulls on it as hard as she can. As Diamond is pulling on the toy, she is also growling trying to scare me into releasing it. I know Diamond would never bite me so I just laugh at her. Yet, because she tries so hard I'll let it go and let her think she really scared me into giving it to her. She makes me laugh everyday. You should try it today; make someone laugh out loud by taking time to care.

Lesson 9

A New Owner

Diamond was given to me years ago when my friend's daughter was having her first child. They did not know how Diamond would act around the baby so they needed to find her a new home. They would keep Diamond in the house at night but she stayed outside during the day. Diamond never went riding around with them as she does with me. She has fun playing with me and she just has really grown on us. Everyone that knows me also knows Diamond for she goes with me daily. Diamond's old owner wanted her back after the child was eight years old. I agreed to let her go back but I missed Diamond very much. After about two weeks, the old owner called saying that Diamond was snapping at everyone in the house and would not eat or drink anything, resulting in her losing weight. She did not want to go back to her old owner and she made sure it was known through her actions.

When we were born, we all were born into sin. Once we gave our lives to the Lord, our sins were forgiven us, for the blood of Jesus paid the price for us to be freed from our sins. The Devil was once our father and owner, but once we give our lives to the Lord, we have a new Father; God become our owner. The Devil is always trying to take us back by feeding us lies and allowing things to come our way to catch our attention. No matter how good he tries to make sin look, do not buy his lies. Everything that looks good is not always good for you. When Jesus went into the wilderness and was tempted by the devil, Satan tried to offer him things that looked good to get Jesus to sin against God. For Him to sin against God would have been Him sinning against Himself for they are one. We too must become one with the Lord. We should never respond to the world in anyway or with anything before we have a talk with the Lord.

During the time that Satan tried to trick Jesus into following him, Jesus had not eaten or drank anything for 40 days and nights. He was physically weak but spiritually strong. He went through everything we could ever go through to show us that we too can endure if we only trust in His word. He really does care for you. He understands your struggles. He knows that your faith is tested on a daily basis. He does not want you to go it alone.

Now that you're a new creation you have to learn how to do everything God's way. While you're learning you will make mistakes, but learn from them and continue your journey with the Lord. Anyone can start things but only those with a will to win will finish. Do not look back to your old owner. Going back will only make you miserable. Keep going forward with the Holy Spirit as your teacher.

God is my father now and He is your father now too. Allow Him to meet your every need on a daily basis. Do not wait until you're in a situation that you cannot get out of to call on Him. He wants to hear from you daily. Anything that you will ever need, He has it. And when you do not understand things, He knows all things. Allow Him to be there for you no matter how big or small the issue may be. When was the last time you had a heart to heart conversation with your heavenly father? He loves to talk to you and He is waiting for you right now. You can be yourself when you talk to Him. You do not have to put up any fronts. There are so many things to appreciate that come along with being a new creature in Christ.

Since you're new, all the old stuff is in your past now. Your new owner has washed them away from you. The Bible says God does not remember your past sins so it's as if you never made a mistake. Since God is not remembering them, why should you? He has given you a chance to start afresh. You may look the same on the outside yet you're not the same. You have been changed inside. As you grow in Christ, that change will begin to show up strongly on the outside.

Diamond looked the same to her old owner yet Diamond had changed. She had fallen in love with her new owners. You can do the same thing; fall in love with God so that when the old owner of your soul tries to take you back, he will find you do not even remember him any more. Right now work through your development so that God can help you have a strong foundation. When anything goes wrong in your life don't allow Satan to make you think God does not love you. He does love you, yet we all have a cross to carry. He told us in His word that we would go through things in this life. He also told us that He would be there with us when they happen. It's so good to know that He is there with us when we're sick or lonely. God is faithful!

Diamond loved her old family when she was with

them but after she came into a new home with a new family she did not want to go back. If a dog can tell when she is in the right place with the right one, we need to wake up and smell the coffee too. You have come too far to look back now. All roads with God have one way signs. If you turn around, you'll be in violation of God's life lines and will have to pay the price for driving the wrong way. Do not lose any sleep over your old father; he is only trying to be like God. Since he is not the real father anything that he does will never be as nice or reach perfection.

Therefore if any man be in Christ, he is a new creature: old things are passed away; behold, all things are become new. – II Corinthians 5:17-18

And all things are of God, who has reconciled us to Himself by Jesus Christ, and has given to us "the ministry of reconciliation".

Your light afflictions, which are but for a moment,

came to strengthen you, not weaken you. Do not look at the things that are seen in the natural, but focus on the things which you cannot see for they are eternal. Everything that you can see is temporal. Why should you lose hope over temporary things? Walk in the spirit of newness and when you get up in the morning remind yourself that it's a new day! Don't carry yesterday's hurts with you into the new day. Determine it to be a new season for you and your loved ones. Yesterday has come and gone; there is nothing you can do to change it or bring it back. Tomorrow is not promised and no one knows the day nor the hour when the Son of God shall return, but today is here right now! If you live it worrying about the past or thinking about the future then you miss out on today.

Lesson 10

The Life Line

Diamond follows me wherever I go. She can be asleep downstairs while I'm sitting in the living room, however, as soon as I get up she awakens and looks up to see if I'm leaving the room, and if so, she follows me. When I get up to go to the rest room she will get up and follow me to the bathroom door. When I come out of the bathroom she is right there at the door waiting for me to come out. My husband says when I have gone somewhere that I could not take her, she lays in her bed crying for me, and paces back and forth to the window waiting for me to return. Any time I leave her in the car with a friend while I go into a store they're so happy when I get back; they tell me Diamond cries for me while I'm gone. She brings joy to my life and I must do the same for her. She is connected to me when we're apart. I wonder what she is doing and I'm sure she wonders when I'm coming home.

My husband and I work for the same company but in different buildings. This allows us to ride to and from work together everyday. When we pull up in the driveway she is already in the window looking out for us to come into the house. When I get in the house she jumps up and down and runs around with joy and excitement. I desire her love, and she desires mine because her life is connected to me.

Abide in Me, and I in you. As the branch cannot bear fruit of itself, except it abide in the vine; no more can you, except you abide in Me. – John 15:4

Jesus goes on to say to us that He is the vine and that we're the branches and because we abide in Him we will be able to bring forth much fruit, however without Him we can do nothing. This is how Diamond reacts when I'm not with her. We bear much fruit and glorify God when we stay connected, according to the scriptures. However, if we do not stay connected to the life line of Jesus, we cannot do anything.

When I think about that, I think about a surge protector. When you plug your computer or anything else into a surge protector you can turn on the computer all day long with the power button on your computer, however, if the surge protector is not on or plugged into a working outlet or socket, you will not be able to do anything with the computer because the main source of power has not been turned on. Sadly this is the position of many people in church today. They attend church, however, they're not plugged into the main power source so they have no power. Nothing changes in their lives. They find themselves in the same position they were in the year before and the year before that, plus the year before the other year and so on. When you're really connected to the true life line, fruit should grow and be evident in your life. If there is no fruit in your life, one of the causes may be, you have to be planted first and then watered, so you can grow strong enough to produce. Many of us will not plant ourselves in the same church long enough to be watered to grow so that we can be strong enough to produce fruit. As soon as someone does something that you do not like or says something that you disagree with, you uproot yourself and move to another church. I thought that you were to go to church for fellowship with God as a church body. If it's all about God, then whatever people do should not move you. This is why it doesn't bother me if a church is so big that the pastor may not know my name. I'm not there to develop a personal relationship with my pastor; I'm there to develop my relationship with the Lord.

My pastor has been ordained by God to preach the word, reprove, rebuke, exhort and teach. I do not see anywhere in the Bible that it tells us to go to church to develop a relationship with the pastor. We're to assemble on one accord with praise and thanksgiving to God. While we're there, the word encourages us to share testimonies to help each other overcome in the world. The Bible tells us not to forsake coming together.

The word of God also tells us that we overcome with the word of God and our testimonies. Why testimonies and not just the word of God? Testimonies confirm God's word; they serve as evidence that God said it, I believe it, and God did just what He said He would. It builds others up when they're weak in faith. It encourages someone else that maybe going through the same thing. God sits up high yet He loves us here below.

When you're connected to the true life line, power failure is never an issue. God is the vine dresser and He Himself prunes you to make sure you will bring forth more fruit. Stay connected to the true life line by staying focused on Him. Look for Him everyday as Diamond does me, wait for Him to show up when you pray to Him. He says in His word if you seek Him you will find Him. When He does show up tell Him how much you love Him with your actions in His presence.

Lesson 11

Endure Until the End

Diamond is a old dog; she has been around for a long time. Due to her age she will sometimes have seizures. The vet gave us some pills to put in her food that would help stop the seizures from happening so many times, the Vet informed us that the bills would not stop them completely. The medicine did no good because Diamond rejected the pills. Once she recognized them in her food, she would push the pills aside and simply enjoy her meal. We were able to get about four or five pills into her system but after that, she would not take the medi-

cine at all. Whenever Diamond does have a seizure she is in a lot of pain. I want to hold and pet her to try to make her feel better, but if I do that it causes her more pain, so as much as I want to, I cannot.

When I go to church for prayer, Diamond comes along with me. One day while I was in prayer at the alter Diamond yelped very loudly. I opened my eyes to see she had leapt in the air, and then she came down fast onto her side in the midst of another seizure. This seizure was not like any one I'd witnessed before and I knew the pain was greater, for this time it had hit her so hard that it caused her to jump in the air and then she was unable to stand. She was on her side breathing hard with her legs stretched out in the air. The episode lasted for about five minutes but it seemed like hours, and I could do nothing but cry; I thought this attack would take her from me. She was in so much pain that I called my husband to see if he thought we should have her put to sleep. As I shared my thoughts with Ricky, Diamond came out of the seizure stood on her feet and waged her tail then she jumped up on me ready to go walking as if nothing had ever happened. Although the seizure was very painful for Diamond once it was over it was over. It was as if Diamond knew what I had just said on the phone to my husband. I picked her up and hugged her telling her how much I loved her and at the same time she was showing me how much she loved me by kissing me.

It has been at least 6 months since Diamond has had a seizure. If I would have taken her to the vet to have her put to sleep I would have missed out on all the joy she continues to bring into my life everyday. From this experience with Diamond she showed me that we give up to soon.

Sometimes we look to other people to help us go through the pain we go through in life but in some of our most painful experiences no one can help us but God. Although we're hurting, we must learn to never give up no matter how painful or how bad the situation seems. We say God is able but when God does not move when we think He should or how we think He should, too often we're ready to throw in the towel. We cannot allow what's going on in the world today to shake our faith in God. Psalm 37:19 tells us:

They (the righteous) shall not be ashamed in the evil time: and in the days of famine they shall be satisfied.

Verse 28 of the same chapter tells us He will not forsake His saints. When things seem to be out of our control, God is still in control. I know people today that will not speak to someone that hurt them years ago. When you hold on to the hurt it will make you bitter and sick. No one will want to be around you because your negativity will pull them down. Learn to get over the pain so you can enjoy the rest of your life.

I have a visual aid board that I made last year. On the board I put a picture of a couple on the beach enjoying the setting of the sun, a couple going for a ride in a cart pulled by a horse, another couple sailing, and pictures of other things I'm believing God for in life. When I look at the board it makes me happier than I was before I took a look at it. The board reminds me of visions and dreams for my life. Many of the things on the board have come to pass but there are some things that have not come to pass yet. Should I give up on them just because they have not happened yet? No, I cannot give up and neither can you. You have to continue to believe and press forward in faith. God will help you complete anything you start yet you have to finish your part.

Whenever I take Diamond outside to walk her, we have to walk by my husband's truck, which he parks close to the walk way. The space is tight but Diamond will stay on the walk way. I will have to step in the grass to get by but not Diamond; she stays on track. Stay on track no matter what happens to you in life. Again, Diamond knows that I will guide and direct her if she is going the wrong way or if she is going into a place that will hurt her in any way. Whenever I go walking for exercise I take Diamond to go with me. Sometimes I can tell she is tired but if I've not completed my workout, I will let her get in the car to wait until I'm ready to go home. She is tired yet when I put her in the car she will bark until I let her out again. I know she is tired and she knows she is tired but because I'm still going, she does not want to quit. She endures with me until the end.

God knows when you're tired but He has not called you home yet, therefore He has not stopped believing in you. You're not finished yet; get out of the car and begin to walk out the vision God has given you for your life. Whenever I get ready to walk Diamond she will turn her body to the side and hold her face up so that I can hook the chain to her collar. Position yourself to be lead by the Lord and then endure to the end. Know that your steps are ordered by the Lord. Listen for His still soft voice.

Lesson 12

High Praise

Every time I come home Diamond greets me at the door. She always jumps up and down when I walk in. She leaps for joy just to be in my presence. I can be very tired from working all day but when she shows me so much love it causes me to bend down and kiss her no matter how tired I may feel. What gets me with Diamond is that no matter how long I have been gone she will always greet me the same way. I do not know how she knows when it is me versus it being someone else at the door but she knows. She will begin to cry for me as soon as my car pulls up. When it is someone else Diamond will bark, but for me she cries in anticipation of my coming in, because she cannot wait to be in my presence. Sometimes she makes me feel so loved that I will go get her a treat before I do anything else.

Praise moves God the same way. He loves for us to praise Him and to give thanks unto His name. We're told to seek first the Kingdom of God. When we do this, all other things shall be added to us. What this is really telling us is that God will take care of our every need. Too often we allow the problems of this world to steal our praise. Praise is very powerful against our enemy. When we praise God it sets an ambush against the enemy.

God says we should know His voice so that we will not follow a stranger. You must stay focused when you begin to praise the Lord. People or things can distract you if you do not learn to stay focused. I love the story about the woman of Canaan that cried out to the Lord to have mercy on her, for her daughter was miserably demon possessed. When she cried out to the Lord He did not answer her at first. She called Him the Son of David and his disciples asked Jesus to send her away. Jesus did not send her away but he responded to her telling her that He was sent to the lost sheep of the house of Israel (Matthew 15:24). After the response she received from the Lord, the Bible says she came and worshiped (bowed before) Him asking Him again to help her. Jesus explained what He said to her at first but this time he made sure she understood Him. He tells her that it was not fitting to take the Israelite's bread and give it to her, a Gentile. She, knowing that He spoke only truth, agreed with Him, but makes the point that even dogs are allowed to eat the crumbs which fall from the master's table. Diamond does this all the time with me when I eat at the dining room table. She knows she is not allowed to sit near the table. Yet, she waits for crumbs to fall. She waits patiently and shows me love while she waits by not worrying me.

When the Canaanite woman did this Jesus

honored her faith and granted her request even though it was not the Gentiles' time. The woman gave Jesus praise even when He referred to her as a dog. Her daughter was healed the same hour He spoke it. She also did not allow the way the disciples felt about her stop her from seeking after the Lord's blessings for her daughter. They wanted Him to send her away. Yet she focused on Him and received the healing she desired for her daughter.

In Acts chapter 16 Paul and Silas had been placed in prison. Before they'd been taken to prison, the magistrates tore off their clothes, and commanded them to be beaten. They were placed into the inner prison with their feet firmly fastened. All of this happened because they came across a certain young woman that was possessed with a spirit of divination. She brought her masters much profit by fortune telling. She began to follow Paul and Silas crying out saying that they were servants of the Most High God showing the way of salvation. All she said was true yet, the wrong (evil) spirit was proclaiming it. Paul became grieved about it because she did this for several days. He turned to her and commanded that the spirit that was operating in her come out in the name of Jesus. The girl was delivered that same hour. When her masters saw that their hope of gain was gone they became mad, caught a hold of Paul and Silas and brought them to the rulers, saying to the magistrates that they exceedingly troubled their city teaching customs that were not lawful to receive nor observe.

At midnight while they were in prison they both prayed and sang songs of praise unto the Lord. They did not pray and sing songs of sorrow about their beating or their bands - the Bible says they sang praises to God. Yes, you read right; not just one song of praise but praises with an S on the end. How powerful is that to read and know? They had their clothes torn off their bodies; they were whipped with lashes and had their feet tightly fastened in prison, yet at midnight, hurting and covered in blood from the lashes, they sang praises unto God. All the prisoners heard them so they couldn't have been singing quietly and without strength. They had to have been singing out with power and authority. Their praise moved God so greatly that it caused an earthquake. The foundations of the prison were shaken causing all the doors to open and every prisoner's bands to become loosed. The keeper of the prisoners called for light. He came trembling and fell down before Paul and Silas asking them what he had to do to be saved. After they told him, they were taken in, washed up and allowed to baptize the guard and his immediate family. He then took them to his house and fed them, rejoicing over his new belief in God. When it was day Paul and Silas were released from prison.

What powerful true stories the Lord has given in the word of God. When you read them it uplifts your spirit and it helps to renew your mind. There are not many of us here in the United States that have been beaten for the sake of Christ. We must learn to praise Him regardless of life's trials and tribulations.

Command your soul to bless the Lord; command your feet, hands, and body to bless the Lord. He desires it and He deserves it even the more.

Lesson 13

Know your Territory

There are a lot of cats in the neighborhood where my church is located. The cats live in the neighborhood but Diamond claimed the neighborhood as her territory. Whenever a cat would come walking in the area, if Diamond was outside she would chase it. I would call her back but she would go after the cat so fast and hard that she could not stop. The cats would all run away from her, then Diamond would come back wagging her tail with her head up high. I would tell her to leave the cats alone; after all, it is their neighborhood but she would not listen to me. Diamond chased the cats so often, it got so that when the cats saw me drive up they would begin to run before Diamond could get out of the car. Then two Siamese cats moved into the neighborhood.

"Diamond there are some new cats in the neighborhood and they will not be scared of you," I warned her. Of course she didn't listen to me at all. One day they were walking around in their community when I got to the church with Diamond. She saw the new cats walking, and no sooner than I let her out of the car, she took off after them. The Siamese cats did not run from Diamond, so I stood there to see the outcome. When Diamond ran barking up to one of them both cats stopped walking and faced Diamond. As Diamond got closer to them they pulled their front legs inward which caused their backs to arch upward. Both cats had positioned themselves to attack if they had to, in order to protect themselves. Diamond's hard bark became a low soft one, and she turned around and came back across the street with her

tail tucked between her back legs. I laughed so hard that I almost wet on myself!

When I finished laughing the Holy Spirit began to minister to me about the whole thing. We as children of God need to start doing the same thing the Siamese cats had done to Diamond – know and defend our territory.

These two cats reminded me of Caleb the son of Jephunneh and Joshua the son of Nun. In Numbers chapter 14 God had instructed Moses to send men to search (explore) the land of Canaan, which God had given to the children of Israel. Moses was to send a man of every tribe, not just any man but leaders. All the men that were selected to go were rulers in their tribes. Moses gave them instruction to assess the land, the people, and the cities, to be of good courage, and bring back fruit from the land. The men did everything that Moses had instructed them to do, however, when Caleb speaks up he tells the congregation that they should go up at once to occupy the land which the Lord had given them for they were well able to overcome it. The other men that went with him (except Joshua) spoke against Caleb's report. They discouraged the congregation so badly that the people wanted to make a captain that would lead them back into Egypt. God had given them the land; all they had to do was go occupy it like Caleb had told them yet they provoked the Lord. Moses and Aaron fell on their faces before the entire congregation, and Joshua and Caleb rent their clothes and spoke to the people trying to get them to see that the land was good. Also Caleb and Joshua referred to the people in the land as bread for them. Still the congregation would not listen; instead they wanted to stone them. When it was all said and done, the men that went up to spy the land which the Lord had given the Israelites who would not come into agreement with Joshua, Caleb, Moses, and Aaron, and the congregation that followed the men that brought back the evil report were not allowed to go into the promised land. They died in the wilderness. Do not die without going to occupy what the Lord your God has given you.

Diamond's size did not scare the Siamese cats because they knew it was *their* new home. Diamond's bark did not scare them because they knew what they were empowered to do together as one body. You see Diamond ran after one cat first, but the other one did not leave it; it stayed right there ready to help defend themselves and their land. When we come together as people of God regardless of our color or gender we will have a bigger impact on earth for the Kingdom of God.

Would you like to get to heaven and have the Lord show you all the things He had given you on earth yet you never claimed them? You allowed your gender, race, lack of profession to stop you. When you walk in faith, God will make sure you have everything you need to fulfill whatever it is you have to accomplish.

Solomon was given the task of building a house for the Lord. King David had already prepared a hundred thousand talents of gold, silver, brass, iron, timber, stone and workmen in abundance to work with him. King David had also commanded all the princes of Israel to help Solomon build the house of the Lord and to bring the Ark of the Covenant along with the holy vessels of God into the sanctuary of the Lord. Solomon had to get the job done yet God had David to set it up. King David did set it up. Yet, he told Solomon something very important in I Chronicles chapter 22; King David told Solomon that only Jehovah could give him wisdom, understanding and charge concerning Israel. Only God can give us the wisdom and understanding we will need to complete any task He gives us, so we should always turn to Him for understanding and direction. Once He tells us to possess something, we cannot allow what we see with our natural eyes to stop us from doing just what He has told us to do for His glory to be revealed in our lives.

I will never forget the first time I had to minister the word of God at this church program that would be viewed live on local television. The Holy Spirit gave me a word for that church and I had to put on 12 robes in order to deliver the word properly. When I came out of the bathroom at the church, the member that had invited me saw me with all the robes on and she became very nervous. She reminded me that they were going to be on live. I thanked her for telling me and moved forward with my mission. There was also a young preacher that came along with me who asked if I was sure I understood what she had just said. I could see in his eyes that he was nervous too. The pastor of the church told both of them (in faith) "it will be alright." He did not know what I was going to do but the man was a man of faith.

When I began to minister the word which the Lord gave me, I began to peel away the robes. Each robe represented issues we face in life. As I took off each robe, the people could feel the level of anointing increasing as the presence of God helped free everyone in the building. One of the elderly deacons of my church also came with me. He cried almost through the whole sermon. When we were on our way back home, he explained to me that he could not stop crying for he felt like something or someone was carrying him, helping him to drop all his issues. I will never forget it for many of the people did not even want to leave the presence of God.

On the night that I was ordained as a minister, God did something very supernatural. When my pastor told me it was time for me to get ordained, I said "Ok. What is that, pastor?" He laughed at me then explained the difference in being a licensed minister then being ordained. He also told me that others had come to him asking to be ordained but I had never done that. I didn't even know the difference. I just knew God had called me. I was the first black female to be ordained in the area. I was making history and did not even know it. People came from all over the world for this service. I would be questioned in front of the congregation, so my pastor took me in the back to go over some of the questions with me, but I was so nervous, I kept getting them all wrong. (He told me after it was all over that I scared him too but he did not want me to know because he did not want to make me more nervous.) The church was filled; people were even standing out side of the church trying to get in.

When I was asked questions during my ordination, I had to not only answer the questions but give a scripture to back up my answer. Now before, I was getting the questions wrong, but now, the correct answers and the scriptures were rolling out of my mouth so fast majority of the congregation stood on their feet in amazement. You see when God has something for you, nothing can stop you when you seek God for wisdom and understanding. The council stopped the questioning, saying I had answered enough perfectly and sharply to their satisfaction. The church went wild they could not believe that they'd stopped the questioning so soon.

That was amazing enough but God was not done yet. You see the church I went to was in a location where many did not support female preachers. When word got out that my pastor was ordaining me there were nasty articles in the paper about him. He did not tell me about it however, I found out about it after everything was done. God did not even let me find out until after the ceremony for He knew I would have allowed that to stop me from doing what I was told to do by my pastor. I'm sure whoever wrote the article was right there in the church during the service.

After the word was preached, the call for salvation went forth. Sometimes I think we rush through the most important part of the service. When the guest preacher finished giving the call I felt a pull to get up out of the chair where I was sitting in front of the pulpit. I knew God wanted it to be reopened. Would they rebuke me or revoke what they had just given me for moving out of place? I did not know, however that did not matter right then. All that mattered was that someone needed Jesus in their life and just maybe that would have been their last chance before they were called from life on earth. When I got up and asked if I could say something, I made the call again in faith. When I began to speak, the supernatural began to manifest. One lady testified that as I was speaking she saw stars dancing around in a circle before her face. Another said someone pushed her forward, yet, no one had touched her at all. Four people came forth and gave their lives to the Lord and the testimonies were still coming forth weeks after about what someone had experience during that second call for salvation. God placed his seal of approval on the whole service. I bless His holy name.

When you go forth in faith know that God has already gone before you, therefore, He knows what you will need when you go forth in faith. Stay in the will of God and listen to the voice He has ordained to speak into your life, as well as keep your personal devotion with the Lord your God. As you draw near to Him He will draw near unto you.

Lesson 14

Lean on Him

Whenever we're in the car, truck or van riding, Diamond can always sense when we are getting ready to cross a bridge or go inside of a tunnel. As we get closer and before we get there, she will run under my feet and lean her whole body on me or jump in my lap. Diamond knows that if she can get to me, she will be fine. I do not know how she knows a bridge is coming or a tunnel is next but she senses a change is about to happen, therefore, she makes sure she is leaning on me.

When we try to make sense out of things we can mess things up. Why tell people your situation when they're in the same situation as you? You need to go to someone who can help. God is always able to help us yet, too often we choose not to lean on Him. Proverbs 3:5-6 says

Trust in the Lord with all you heart and lean not to your own understanding. In all your ways acknowledge Him, and He shall direct your paths.

We have to learn how to trust God with everything that concerns us. He is our creator. Surely, the Creator knows how to take care of His creation.

Once David and his men were out of the city (1 Samuel 30) when they came back they found the city burned down and their wives, sons, and daughters had been taken captive. The Bible says David and the people that were with him wept until they could not weep any more. David was grieved, just as the men that were with him. The men spoke of stoning David for their souls were grieved for their families. This caused David to be come greatly distressed. What did David do when the men turned against him? He did what we all need to do when others come against us; David encouraged himself in the Lord. What this is saying is that he strengthened himself in Jehovah Elohim. David asked the priest to bring him the priestly garment. Once it was brought to him, David inquired of the Lord about pursuing after the troop that had taken their families and burned the city. Jehovah told him to pursue after them and not only did the Lord tell him to pursue, Jehovah also told him what the outcome would be:

Pursue: for you shall surely over-take them, and without fail recover all – I Samuel 30:8

If you read on, you will see that they did just as the Lord said they would; they recovered all! Do you remember how safe you felt when you were little and someone you could trust would pick you up and throw you up in the air? You did not want them to stop. You would smile, laugh, scream and cry out for them to do it again. We knew they would not let us fall. We knew we were in safe hands. What we did not know as a child was that they could have messed up and not caught us by mistake. God never makes mistakes. We can trust Him with our lives. He knows what's best for us and He will not withhold any good thing from us. What I love about God is when I talk to Him I do not have to worry about Him telling my business to anyone. I can talk to Him and be real.

Diamond also comes to me at home when my grandchildren are there. She realizes that they are little so she is very careful around them. They sometimes play too hard with her and she knows she cannot hurt them. When she gets tired of them pulling on her, she doesn't snap at them - she just runs out of the room into another room away from them. If they follow her and will not leave her alone then

Diamond will run under my legs knowing I will make them stop. She knows I will not allow them to hurt her. Sometimes I think Diamond is the smartest one in the house.

No matter what you go through in life, learn to lean on God your father with everything. Do not wait until things are all out of order. Lean on Him with the little things as well as the big things. Talk to Him about everything for he longs to fellowship with you. David's men turned their backs on him when things did not go the way they thought they should but God was still there with David, and when no one else was willing to take up for him God stepped in. Allow Him to step into your situation right now. There is nothing too hard for Him. If you have the will, God has the way. His grace and His mercy are on your side. He will not allow you to fall into the enemy's hands. God will step in right on time all the time, so trust Him with all that concerns you. Remember He knows us from end to beginning, not our beginning to our end but our end to our beginning. This means He already knows the outcome of everything, every issue, every mountain you must cross, every valley you must go through.

When David and his men returned to see that the enemy had taken their families, it looked like defeat. It looked like they had lost. Yet, it was just a golden opportunity to see the hand of the Lord move on their behalf. If God never allows unfortunate things to come our way then we will never know what He is able to do on our behalf.

I had to have an operation that should have only been a two day stay in the hospital. I did go home in two days but I had to go right back into the hospital the same night I came home. I could not keep anything down and I was in a lot of pain. I ended up staying in the hospital for a week and a half longer. My organs had to be removed and put back during my operation. The doctor explained to me that when they put my organs back in, they did not lay right. This caused an upset inside of me where my organs would not function properly; they wanted to be back in place. It was explained to me that it was just like a water hose with a kink in it. When the hose has a kink in it, water cannot flow out fast. Have you ever tried to wash your car or truck and had that happen to you? The water wouldn't come out fast due to the kink in the hose. To get the kink out you will pull on the hose and try to fix the kink so that the water can flow properly. That is what my organs were doing inside of me; they're trying to get the kinks out so that they could flow properly. This was a very painful experience and I truly had to lean on the Lord. My doctor told me that I could help to get the kinks out by walking which was even more painful. When I would walk, I would hurt even the more. Yet, it was helping to fix the problem inside of me. What seemed to be hurting me even more was really helping me to heal.

Diamond does not like taking a bath. She will run from me and even try to hide when it's bath time. Even though she does not like taking baths she knows I would never do anything to hurt her so when I do finally catch her and place her in the tub she will stand still and allow me to bathe her.

We have to be willing to do whatever the Holy Spirit leads us to do knowing that even when we do not understand, God would not have us to do anything that is not for our own good. Friends would call and some even came by to see me with flowers and gifts, however, there was nothing they could say or do to help relieve me from the pain I was in. My husband and children could not even help me. Only God my father could help me endure the pain. I had to lean on Him knowing that His word was true, for He promised never to leave us nor forsake us and I believed Him. He will make away out of no way for you. He will turn your darkest night into a brighter day. God will give you back your joy and renew your strength. God can supply your need because God is an awesome God. He can do the impossible and the incredible; He can perform miracles. He reigns with all power and there is nobody like Him. Trust Him with what concerns you. He is the King of Glory, strong and mighty in battle. If you lean on Him you will never be displeased with His protection or His guides. I was able to follow my doctor's instructions because I trusted the One that had given him the wisdom and knowledge to be able to do what he was doing as a doctor. The greatest doctor ever was the real One in control.

Lesson 15

Unmovable Faith

Diamond is a small dog mixed with pit bull. My next door neighbors have a big dog, and for some reason they just do not get along. Everyday that I walk Diamond, she and the neighbor's dog will always bark at each other. Diamond is a house dog. She has been inside since we got her but the neighbor's dog stays outside. One day my daughter was walking Diamond and the neighbor's dog broke loose. Neither Diamond nor my daughter saw the dog coming until it was too late. The dog attacked Diamond from the back. My daughter was pulling

Diamond . . . A Girl's Best Friend

Diamond by the chain trying to get her away from the other dog. She could not fight back because of the chain was pulling her away and when it was all over Diamond had a couple of bruises. My daughter picked her up once the neighbors retrieved their dog. Instead of Diamond being afraid, after the attack, everyday as we walked her she tried to get to the other dog. You would think she would try to stay away from the other dog but she did just the opposite. She would try so hard to get to the other dog that she would cause her leash to tighten around her neck. Diamond refused to allow her size to stop her from facing her enemy.

On another day afterwards, the neighbors were walking their dog and Diamond was loose on the porch with me and my husband. When Diamond spotted the dog she took off after him. It all happen so fast; she jumped on their dog before I could even say her name. Unlike my daughter, they did not pull their dog away; instead they let the leash go. When they did that, it was on! Diamond was able to avenge herself. When I got to Diamond, the neighbor's dog was not trying to fight back; he was trying to get away from Diamond. I think the neighbor's dog was glad to see me pick Diamond up and take her away. You see, even though he was bigger, it did not mean he was better. Now, when I walk her, Diamond looks at the other dog as if to say, 'you're a joke.' She doesn't even listen to his barking anymore. When he barks at her now Diamond just keeps on walking; she has moved on. She knows that the big dog is just making a lot of noise.

This reminds me of David when he was a young boy. David was young yet he killed a lion with his bare hands. Again and again we read in the word of God how he would face his enemies no matter what the size. I believe Diamond is so brave because she has pit blood mixed in her. While Diamond is mixed with pit, we're also mixed as children of God. Everyone that has given their life to the Lord is mixed with the Holy Spirit. We're mixed with someone stronger than the strength of a pit bull. You have to know what you have been blessed with. We have the gift of the Holy Spirit inside of us. The same power that raised Jesus from the grave is the same power nside of you.

Just like my neighbor's dog, The devil makes a lot of noise trying to scare us yet when we know what we really have inside of us, he does not scare us anymore. Fear is the opposite of faith which is needed to please God. Without faith we cannot please Him. The Bible also teaches us that we cannot do anything without Him. If we do anything without Him, then what we have done is nothing for it was done without Him. We should always try our best to walk in faith. When the devil tries to get us to speak negatively we must paralyze our mouth to negativity and speak faith. I know you're saying that it's easier said than done. We will mess up a lot of times but it's just like when we spill something on the floor - we get up and clean it up as soon as possible so that it will not dry up and stain. We need to do the same thing when we mess up with our faith. When we speak something out of faith we need to reverse it as soon as possible with positive faith-filled words. Hold fast to the pattern of sound words which you have learned in the word of God in faith.

When Abraham was blessed with a son by God at an old age God told him to take his son up a mountain and to offer him as a sacrifice to Him. God did not want Abraham to really kill his son; He wanted him to love and trust Him more then anything or anyone. When Abraham got to the mountain side he told those with him to wait at the bottom of the hill while he and his son went up and they would return. Abraham spoke in faith! He knew if God would have him to do what he had told him to do, then He was able to also cause him to live again. His faith was strong enough to believe God when he did not understand Him. Even though Abraham did not understand why God would have him offer his son he walked and spoke in faith believing God would provide a lamb for the sacrifice.

We do not have to know how God is going to do

whatever we believe Him for. We just have to know that whatever He does will be for our best. Speak life to your situation and know that all things are working together for your good, for greater is He that is in you then he that is in the world. You have the ability and the power to come out on top. Faith looks beyond what you can see with your natural eyes and believes what you do not see but what you know to be true. When you go to sit down in a chair you never check to see if the chair will hold you first, you just sit down. It's the same when you're ready for bed at night; you don't check to see if the bed will hold your weight first. You could be in a hotel ready to lay in a bed that you've never been on before yet, you do not check to see if the bed will hold you before getting on it. This is how your faith should work on a daily basis. No matter what the enemy brings your way, you should always walk in faith not allowing him to cause you to lose focus. God is able to do exceedingly above what we can ask or even think, and it's according to the power that works inside of us.

Some of the people that were hit by the storm Katrina in Louisiana came back to rebuild their homes. Many were asked why would they rebuild when another Katrina could come back again. Their replies were, "because this is home; we're not going to allow fear to cause us to leave home." I heard one man say that he would rebuild over and over again because it's home to him. So many of us give up if things do not work out the way we think they should at first. If things don't work out that first time, start all over with another plan until one of them works. I have learned that mistakes turn out to be opportunities for improvement. You can learn from your mistakes and cause change to improve the lives of many people. God has not given you the spirit of fear and since God has not given it to you then you do not have to accept it.

The walk of faith is allowing God to carry you. Allow Him to order your steps knowing He is able to keep you from falling. You would not need faith if everything was mapped out for you step by step.

No matter what, stay in faith knowing that God will be pleased with you for not doubting in the midst of your test of faith.

Esther in the Bible went in to see the King without being called by the King which could have cost her her life but she knew she had to go in and talk to him to save her people. Her stance was, "If I perish let me perish I'm going to see the King." She did what she had to do in order to save the lives of many. If Esther would have allowed the spirit of fear to rule her she would have never stepped out in faith. What is fear trying to hinder you from doing? What has the spirit of fear caused you to lose? Take it all back in faith. Go into the enemy's camp and release or reject the fear and take back everything that has been stolen from you. Speak it in faith and watch God help you reclaim it.

Lesson 16

Change

While my husband was cutting the grass in our front yard, one of the mower blades threw a rock which hit the storm door causing the glass to break. Our neighbor helped him remove the broken pieces, and they made sure that no glass was left on the front porch that the grandchildren could get a hold of and hurt themselves. I waited until they had removed all the glass before I called Diamond to walk her. When I opened the front door, I tried to get Diamond to jump through the open section of the storm door. She would not jump through the middle. After I walked her, I opened the storm door plus the front door to let her in the house. Once Diamond went in the house, I left the front door open so I could check the mail box out front. Diamond came and stood at the storm door crying for me. I told her she could come to me but Diamond was so use to not being able to get out while the glass was there. She could not tell the reason she was able to see me more clearly was because the glass was not in place. I called her about five times yet, because she was use to the glass being there she wouldn't budge, but waited for me to come inside.

Changes in the economy have forced some organizations to change the way they do business. Resistance to change may be rooted in the fear of failure. Routine, predictable manner is comfortable; it's the normal way of doing things. Many resist change simply because it is unfamiliar. Change is not always bad on my job. The changes that have been made so far have given some people more responsibility and with the added responsibility came more experience. The more experience you have the better your resume looks. For some coworkers the added work caused them to quit. For me, pulling more ability out of me makes me a better person. We have to remember knowledge is powerful! You can take what you learn and use it for your benefit.

I was blessed to work one summer for a millionaire as a nanny for his grandchildren. Maybe to someone else, being a nanny is not much of a blessing, however, I love children so it was a blessing for me. The additional blessing was to be in the midst of two millionaires, the gentleman and his wife, and to be able to explore their territory. I learned a lot from watching them. He was laid back and very friendly. If you did not know him personally, you would have never known he was a millionaire. The wife was more high class. She carried herself well and stayed in shape. What amazed me was they used a lot more wisdom with everything than the people in the church. When I left there, I changed the way I did a lot of things in life. The more I saw them do things differently and better, the more I wanted to change.

I will never forget how he handled one of his workers stealing gas from him. The yard workers that took care of the estate would fill up the work truck he owned. One of the workers took the credit card and was filling his car up every week. I was in the kitchen preparing the children some lunch when he called all the yard workers inside to talk to them. He simply said:

"I know you have been using my card to fill your car. I know who you are and I want it to stop today. Have a nice day and I will see you all tomorrow."

He knew who it was, yet, he called all of them in so that no one would try it again thinking they could continue to get away with it. If he only called the one that was doing the stealing, then he may have never told the others he'd gotten caught. You know misery loves company so to kick it in the butt he called them all.

He had one young worker that habitually came

Diamond . . . A Girl's Best Friend

to work late, and then came to work only when he wanted too. One week, the worker did not come to work until that Friday. The owner of the house called him in and said,

"How are you son; I have not heard from you all week."

When the young man told him he was fine and that he just did not feel like coming to work, the gentleman told him:

"I'm glad you're fine because I would not want to fire you while you're sick. Have a nice life." He kept eating and never looked up at the young man. The young man stood there for about ten minutes. I think he was in shock. He was use to coming to work when he wanted and staying home recovering from his partying and getting away with it. He never expected things to change.

Ron Glassman said, "The brain is the only programmable organ in the body. Choose the direction you want to program yours... and enjoy the journey." This is so true; you have to let go of old pictures you're use to seeing and the old messages you're use to hearing. Now you have to visualize the new pictures over and over again until the new is programmed and becomes your standard. I love to listen to the Bible on CD because it helps me capitalize on what I'm learning. As I listen, my brain is drawing the image of my imagination according to what I hear and perceive.

Lesson 17

From the Pit to the Palace

While walking Diamond in our neighborhood I noticed she would always pull to go down in the ditch. A ditch is dug out and used as drainage for waste. I could not understand why she would want to go in a ditch instead of trotting along on the side of the road or in the grass in the yard. One day I stopped and allowed her to go for whatever she was after in the ditch. Once there, Diamond began to nibble on the grass that grew there. I noticed the beautiful green and vibrant color of the grass that she chewed on, then took note of the grass in the yard, which was only partially green and mixed with brown. Its color didn't compare to the grass in the ditch. I couldn't help but smile when I realized that from my perspective, Diamond was crazy for wanting to go into a ditch, however she knew what she was doing. Even though the ditch carried waste and trash, and smelled bad, something good was growing in the midst of the mess.

Good things can be produced from what seems to be unpleasant surroundings or circumstances. Too many times we as Christians give up when we go through trials in life. Those whom have decided not to choose Jesus Christ as their Lord and savior have no hope, yet those whom have repented for their sins and have confessed Jesus to be the Son of God, allowing Him to be Lord of their lives have more then just hope; we have a promise. Christ has promised us in His word that He will never put more on us than we can bear. The devil's mission is to steal, kill and destroy; he tries to steal your dreams, kill your vision and destroy your future. God created us all with purpose. He has given you a measure of faith to complete that purpose even in the midst of something messy.

We cannot be fooled by Satan's devises. Hebrews 11:6(b) tells us:

God is a rewarder of them that diligently seek Him.

We have to continue to seek and not give up too soon. You have to bewilling to push pass all of your downs to get to the place God has ordained for you to be in life so that He will get the glory out of your life.

Joseph was thrown in a pit by his own brothers. They were jealous of the favor his earthly father showed him. At the same time, Joseph was also favored by God. God would reveal things to him in dreams, but Joseph had a problem with telling everything to his brothers. When God reveals something to us about our future it's not always a good idea to share it with others. Many times we think that those around us love and care for us yet some of them are just waiting for us to fall. After Joseph shared his dreams with his brothers, they began to hate him even more than they already did. They already hated him because their father loved him more. Their hatred ran so deep that they all but one wanted to kill him. Had it not been for a single brother who suggested that rather than take his life, to just throw him in a pit, Joseph would have been dead.

What was indeed a tough situation for Joseph ended up being the very route for bringing his dreams to pass. When you study and read the story about Joseph you will see that he faced many tests and trials, yet he stayed focused and would not allow anything or anyone to shake his faith in God. He was sold into slavery, then placed in jail for something he did not do. Yet, God blessed him to be able to interpret dreams (Genesis 41:16). This gift helped him to get out of jail. Not only did it get him out of jail, it placed him in a high position. Pharaoh placed him over his house, and according to Joseph's words, all the people under Pharaoh were ruled. Pharaoh set Joseph over all the land in Egypt (Genesis 41:41). A gold necklace was placed around his neck; Pharaoh's ring was place on his hand and he was arrayed in fine vestures.

What a story! Joseph came from the pit and ended up in the palace, and so can you. You may be in the pit right now and it may seem that there's no way out. You cannot begin to understand what God is doing in your life. The Bible states that our ways are not God's ways. He thinks higher than us; He knows more than us and He has already seen and knows the end! Trust Him to know what is best for your life and He will get you from the pit to the palace just like He did for Joseph. Joseph's position allowed him to save the lives of his family and his people. What his brothers meant for bad, God meant for good. God allowed those circumstances and events to happen so that Joseph would be in position to save His chosen people during the famine that came over the land for seven years.

If you find yourself in what seems like a ditch or a pit, instead of asking God 'why me' why not ask the Holy Spirit what He would have you to do while you're there? Remember our Lord has no respect of persons; what He does for one He is willing to do for all.

Lesson 18

Be Real

LaToya has a black leather couch set in her living room. While I was in the hospital and LaToya saw after Diamond, I warned LaToya that she would need to cover her furniture to keep Diamond and her shedding hair off of it. To my surprise, LaToya shared with me that Diamond never even attempted to get on her couch, even if LaToya wanted to hold and pet her. After giving it some thought, I realized that LaToya's couch is fake leather, not genuine leather. It only looked authentic, but Diamond could tell that it didn't feel the way it should have felt. Diamond is just a dog, yet, she knows when something is real or not. Diamond was not drawn to be on LaToya's furniture because it wasn't real.

Colossians 3:14 tells us that love is the perfect bond of unity. If we want to walk in perfection we must walk in love. We cannot choose who we will love; our love must be real which means it must be genuine. There are so many fake people that no one sees the differences in a child of God and the children of the world. It should not be this way. People should be able to see our light shining brightly for the Lord. They should not have to read a 'I Love Jesus" tee-shirt to be able to identify you as a child of God. We should have the characteristics of our heavenly father in us and on display. How many people do not want to hear what you have to say about the Lord because they know you're not really walking the walk you talk about? Do they hear you talking about people instead of lifting them up? Words are powerful; the Bible says they are so powerful that life and death are in the power of what we say.

Do others see you worship and praise God but your children hear you talk about everyone in the church when you get home? Corinthians tells us love should never fail; love should remain forever. How can you say you cannot forgive when God says you must walk in love? He would not tell you to do something that you're incapable of achieving. So it's not that you cannot, it's that you do not want to do it. When you really begin to walk in the love of God, you can love anyone. You will be able to bond with them even when your personalities are totally different. In order to win people to the Lord we have to be able to reach them. You cannot reach them without bonding with them. You can smile and look the part but if you're not really living it there will be no bonding.

Super glue does not paste two elements together; it bonds them together by absorbing itself into the elements' surfaces so that the two actually fuse into one. We must become that super glue for the Lord.

We must fuse or melt people to the point that they will be bonded with the Lord. We will become the glue by sharing the love of God, living a godly life before them, giving them time when we do not have the time, and helping them to overcome their strongholds in life. When we draw them to the Lord this way, they will never leave Him because they have been bonded, not pasted.

Having an example of someone who is real makes it so much easier to follow the Lord. In I Samuel, David and Jonathan's love for each other was so real that even when Jonathan's father, King Saul hated David so much that he wanted to kill him, Jonathan went against his father's wishes and remained faithful to David. Chapter 18 of I Samuel says the soul of Jonathan was knit to the soul of David. Jonathan loved David as his own soul. Verse 3 says:

Then Jonathan and David made a covenant, because he loved him as his own soul.

When Saul was determined to kill David, Jonathan and David wept together secretly (I Samuel 20:41) then David departed in peace. This would be the last time they would be together. They made a covenant between them and their descendants. When David is made King he does not forget his covenant with Jonathan. Even when both Saul and Jonathan had been killed, David asked if there were anyone still alive of the house of Saul, to whom he could show the kindness of God for Jonathan's sake. When David learns of Jonathan's lame son Mephibosheth, David sent for him, gave him all the land that belonged to his grandfather, Saul, and assured him that he would eat at his table forever. You see love never fails it just keeps on giving.

Have you ever used imitation vanilla when making a pie or any other dessert? With the real vanilla you would have only had to use a ½ of teaspoon because it's very strong, but if you are using imitation vanilla you have to use almost the whole bottle to try to get close to the same flavor the real vanilla would have given you. The fake stuff is cheaper but it ends up costing you more in the long run. Being fake is the cheap way. Being real, makes you spend time with the Lord. The only way to be more like Him is to get to know Him. Read His word for yourself; learn what He has to say to you. The more you get to know Him the more you will love and trust Him. The more you trust and love Him, the more you will want others to meet Him. Show your real love by being real everyday of your life. He will reward you like no one else can.

Lesson 19

Be Still

My husband and I live in a two story house with our children. Diamond has a bed in our room which is upstairs. She also has a bed in the living room downstairs. She can be at rest in her bed upstairs in our room, yet when I open the cookie jar not just downstairs but also on the opposite side of the house, she still hears it! At the sound of that jar opening, Diamond will come running downstairs in anticipation of receiving a cookie, or at the very least, hoping that I will drop one by mistake, knowing she will be able to have it. I have even tried using *both hands to open the cookie jar in an effort not to make any noise, yet she still hears it and comes running.*

"How do you always hear this jar?" I asked her. She just looked at me wagging her tail and waited for her cookie.

One day when she came down to receive from the cookie jar the Holy Spirit dropped the answer in my spirit that blessed me to change my ways. It made me shift things around in my daily life. Diamond can always hear the cookie jar because Diamond is not constantly running around in circles on a daily basis. Even though she is a dog, she has sense enough to rest. Sometimes, when I'm on the go, Diamond will come with me. If we have been gone all day, when we get back to the house she will go eat and drink, then lay down. When I'm ready to go back out I will call Diamond but if she's tired, instead of running down the stairs she will sit down at the top of the stairwell and look down at me with her tail wagging. I will ask her if she wants to go back out with me, and sometimes her answer is no. Instead of running to me she will stay there as if to say 'it's time for me to rest now; you go right ahead but I need to rest.'

Many times we make ourselves too busy running around doing nothing. When the day is over we're so tired yet we get right back up and start another day of the same repeatable things we did the day before. We can be so busy doing the work of the Lord that we forget to spend time in His presence to receive from Him. There's a story in the Bible about the importance of being still.

Jesus had been invited to Martha's house where Mary also visited. While Martha busied herself with being a perfect hostess, Mary chose what the Bible calls the good part (Luke 10:42). Instead of being preoccupied with the duties of hosting guests, Mary sat with the others to listen to Jesus' teaching, which Martha was not happy about. Her expectation was that Mary help her. When Martha complained to Jesus about Mary not helping her as a hostess, the complaint caused her to receive a teaching rebuke from the Master Himself. He tells her that she is too anxious and troubled over many things. It is important that we don't allow ourselves to become bogged down and so busy that we can't rest and become refreshed in the presence of God. Just like Martha wanted Mary to assist her, you may run into situations where your friends or even family call and request your help or want you to go somewhere with them. They may even be willing to pay for your lunch, dinner etc. You have to know when it's time to say no or no thank you, so that you can take your daily medicine, called rest.

I will never forget a time years ago that I was so tired I could not rest properly. I was a youth leader, on the usher board, heading the young adult choir and the jail ministry, an associate minister, wife, and mother, plus I was working full time. When I went to bed one night, I said to God in prayer that I was tired and needed refreshing. I will never forget that night. I went to sleep as soon as my head touched the pillow.

In my sleep I heard this beautiful music and singing. It was nothing like I had ever heard before in my life. I knew I was not listening to any music here on earth. God was allowing me to hear the angels sing! I felt the love and comfort from their words to God. When they stopped singing I woke up. I tried to wake my husband up to tell him what had just happened but he was in a deep sleep. I felt so refreshed, so renewed, so filled with energy that I got up and tried to write down the words I heard on an index card; then I went back to bed rejoicing and fully refreshed. The next day, I looked for the index card but could not find it, nor could I remember the words that I'd heard in the song. I do not believe it was meant to be written or heard by anyone else. God was honoring my words by helping me to rest. When we're weak, He is always strong and knows what we need even before we ask.

When was the last time you visited that quiet place and just lay in the presence of the Lord, not asking Him for anything but just listening to Him and allowing Him to refresh and restore you? No distractions, no one to take your focus away from God - just you and Him? I'm not talking about simply going to church or Bible study. Most of us have that down perfectly. We will be there in body but be so tired that we're not there in spirit. I'm talking about that quiet place, your secret closet, where there is no one else but you and God. We can sometimes be in church, and random thoughts will have our minds drifting then focusing on everything that we have to do when we leave church. We're there but we're not there. If you're in leadership, you may be there but you have so many responsibilities that you're not able to be still. We even sit and worry about tomorrow while in church. Why are we the children of the Most High God anxious about anything? God says, in so many words to us that we need to learn how to take a chill pill.

Be still and know that I am God – Psalm 46:10a

To be anxious is to be fearful of what may happen; it means you're worried. We must remember fear is a spirit which was not sent from God but from the enemy of God.

For God has not given us a spirit of fear, but of power and of love and of a sound mind.
– II Timothy 1:7

If God did not give you the spirit of fear then it is resting on you illegally. That spirit is trespassing on God's property. As a child of God, you have been bought with the price of Jesus' blood. You belong to God! Tell it to get off of you and never come back! If someone came in your house uninvited and would not leave you would not just say 'okay have your own way.' No, you would make them leave; you'd call the police and have them put out and dare them to come back. You may even pull out a few weapons. You have been fully armed by God to declare war on the enemy. Child of God you're armed and dangerous! God has given you the power of His Word which is sharper than any two-edged sword. You have the power of His blood that heals. You have the power of the Holy Spirit that raised Jesus from the grave and you have the power of the name of Jesus which is above every other name. Allow God to get the glory out of your situation by using your power. Whatever you fear or are worried about is not stronger than the tools God has made available to you, so use them to His glory.

Jesus also said that Martha was troubled. Listen to one of Webster's listings for troubled: a condition of ill health, causing pain. Wow! Can you see what this uninvited guest can do to your body? I found out that disease is anything that causes you to be diseased. When you're not resting, you are prone to disease which can both weaken and damage you.

Jesus also tells Martha that Mary has done what was needed. To say that something is needed is to say you cannot make it without it! You can't make it without resting in God and spending time in His presence. You keep telling yourself that one day you'll get yourself together, and one day you're going to put your priorities in order. Stop saying one day and make it today! There is no other way; you must condition yourself to be still. Finish this chapter then go to your secret closet and shut yourself in with God. God wants to bless you with wisdom, knowledge, peace, joy, increased faith and understanding. Will you take the time to be still daily so that you can receive every free gift God has for you, His child? Why not start now? Turn the phone and the television off and put up a 'Do Not Disturb' sign. Play some meditative music and turn the lights down low; sing to the Lord a new song, then talk to your heavenly father and wait in His presence to hear from Him. Add God to your calendar everyday; you will see a difference. Come on; give it a try. What do you have to lose? Absolutely nothing, but you have everything to gain. The enemy knows that if you take the time daily to be still, you will be able to hear from God more clearly. This is why he desires to keep you busy, but let him know you're on to his tricks and enough is enough. Do not allow him to trouble you any more! Kick his butt out of your life - tell fear and worry that they have to go now in Jesus name. Hit the road worry, Hit the road busybody, hit the road fear and don't you come back no more - no more!

Lesson 20

Another way

*D*iamond is used to sitting in the front seat of my van while I drive. We start our drive with her on the passenger side, but at every stop light she will move over to my lap, and then move about the car from the front seat to the back seat during the ride. During one of our outings, I picked up a friend, Deacon Warren Williams, who needed a ride from the auto repair shop. When Deacon Warren got in the van, Diamond moved to the back seat but still sought to get into my lap at every stop light as she was accustomed to doing. As she moved forward *from the back, Deacon Warren tried to prevent her from getting to me and keep her confined to the back, but Diamond knew she was welcomed to my lap. Rather than be hindered by Deacon Williams, Diamond simply used an alternate route to get to where she wanted to be.*

Deacon Williams commented, "She didn't care that I cut off her usual way of getting to her master, she just found another way."

When he said that, something clicked in my spirit. Diamond did not forget that her master time and time again had allowed her to sit in her lap. And now here is was that someone she did not know was trying to keep her from doing what she had always done. Diamond did not allow this strange person or voice to stop her. She didn't even waste her efforts or time barking and yelling; she simply found another way!

As children of God we need to stop allowing life's potential road blocks prevent us from getting to our Master and pursuing our visions, dreams or goals.

God will always help you find your way when you ask of Him (Matthew 7:7-8). We waste so much time trying to prove ourselves or prove a point to someone else when we do not have to prove anything to anyone but God. If there is a will, there is a way for it to come to pass.

When King Herod heard about Jesus being born from the wise men that came from the east to Jerusalem to worship Jesus (Matthew2:1-3), King Herod and all of Jerusalem was troubled. Before allowing them to continue their search for baby Jesus, King Herod informed them to come back and let him know where Jesus was so he could come to worship Him. If you notice in the Bible when the King asked them to bring him word so that he could worship Jesus, there is no response from the wise men. The Bible simply says,

When they heard the King they departed –
Matthew 2:9

The wise men were later divinely warned in a dream that they should not return to King Herod. The Bible states:

They departed for their own country another way – Matthew 2:12.

King Herod did not stop them from going home; they listened to the divine warning and went home another way. Their destination was reached and the purpose of their trip was fulfilled. The King in authority on earth was not able to override or change their plans to worship the Son of God and go home. Just because someone has a higher position than you does not mean they are always right. We must know the voice of the Lord (John 10:3-5). Pray for the gift of discernment so you will know when something is of God and when it is not of God. The wise men did what they had come to do and returned back to their homeland another way.

There is always another way; when your first

plan does not work don't give up on your dreams, your visions or your goals in life. President Abraham Lincoln exercised perseverance so excellently in his life time. He did not allow any of his failures to stop him from achieving in life. He tried to run his own business twice and failed; he ran for State Legislator but was defeated; even a nervous breakdown did not stop him. I'm sure he took time to recover yet he did not stop. After recovering he ran for Congress twice and both times he was defeated. Lincoln ran for Senate two times but lost each time. Mr. Lincoln even ran for Vice President of the United States but lost. How many of us would have given up after having the nervous breakdown? When plan one does not work have your self a plan two. Sometimes you will need a plan three, four, five, six, seven, eight, nine and ten, etc.... Life will shoot us many blows; how we allow the blows to affect us will determine our outcome. We can see this from Mr. Lincoln's life experience. Because he did not stop, he became the 16th President of the Untied States of America. I can imagine each time Lincoln failed it made him stronger and more determine to achieve. Look at all he tried; even trying different things, he still at the end was met with failure. God had a higher purpose and plan for his life than what Lincoln would have settled for if he would have won any of the other titles.

You have to realize that everyone is not always going to agree or believe in you. You have to listen to what God is saying to you above what any man or woman is telling you. God knows your destiny and He will guide you the right way if you listen to His voice above others. Stop and think about it, are you settling for less than what you were created to accomplish in life? Has God shown you in a dream or vision something other than what you're doing right now? Do not take the potential God has placed in you to the grave; find another way to give birth to it. To get where you have never been, be willing to do what you have never done. Go the extra mile and when you get weary lean on the Lord (Matthew 11:28-30). Take time to hear the voice of the Lord;

study His word and believe it, then you will be able to achieve it. When we put God first in our lives, allowing Him to be the center of our joy nothing will be impossible.

For with God nothing shall be impossible – Luke 1:37

Some TV ministry programs are very good and help spread the good news around the world. But even with that said, you cannot allow TV ministry programs or regular church services to be the only time you hear the word. Start your own devotional fellowship with the Lord. Make sure you have quiet time so you can allow God to minister to your spirit. When you pray don't just end your prayer and leave the presence of God; allow Him to speak to you. Think about it. When you are on the telephone with a friend you don't do all of the talking. You wait and allow the other person to respond to you. In order to hear the other person you make sure that you have the right volume, and there is not a lot of noise in the background. You may even position a pad near you, ready to write down their instructions or directions. We should set the atmosphere for our time with our heavenly father too. God can give you the instructions you need to bring your dream to pass. Every new day is a new opportunity to achieve victory.

Lesson 21

The First Kiss

Every morning I wake up to a nice kiss from Diamond. She can tell when I'm moving to get up. As I turn my head towards the door Diamond is right there kissing me on my hand. She is the first one to say good morning to me when I open my eyes. It makes me feel loved. I know she loves me but love is not only found in words spoken; love is found within our actions. Diamond greets me with true love first thing in the morning and it helps me to start my day with a smile.

When we take the time to kiss the face of our father, we will feel Him spiritually kissing us back. God says in His word that if we seek Him early we will find Him. How do you think God would feel if we that call Him Father would greet Him as soon as we get up in the morning? Not after we have gone to the bathroom to refresh ourselves but as soon as we open our eyes - greet Him with a kiss by turning to Him before we start our busy day. I say good morning to the Holy Spirit and my guiding angels, along with blessing God before I get out of the bed. I thank them all for watching over me while I and my family rested during the night.

With everything that is going on in the world today we should not rise up without seeking the face of God. God is the source of our life and He is the length of our days. When we come to Him, we draw closer to Him and we learn to receive His love. He is God but when you draw close to Him daily He will become a father to you. There will not be a sense of distance, but instead you will feel the closeness.

Psalm 27:1,5 says:

The Lord is my light and my salvation; whom shall I fear? The Lord is the strength of my life; of whom shall I be afraid?

For in the time of trouble He shall hide me in His pavilion: in the secret of His tabernacle shall He hide me; He shall set me up upon a rock.

Psalm 27 is a Psalm of David. He knew no matter what happened in his life, as long as God remained his light and his salvation he didn't have to worry about anything. God is in control and He will lead you. With God as your light He will light up every dark path in your life to help guide you safely. As your salvation He is your deliverer; He will make a way of escape for you when you need one. God tells us:

Seek you My face - Psalm 27:8

Diamond . . . A Girl's Best Friend

David tells God that he will do just that daily. God loves to fellowship with us; He loves the one-on-one relationship. Many lay down at night but do not get up in the morning; many take their own shoes off when their ready for bed but because death has come during the night someone else will put their shoes on them in the morning. Do not wait until you're sick or have to go into the hospital to seek the face of God early. When you're sick you're not always thinking with a clear mind. The pain and situation can cause you to function differently than you would if you were not ill. Begin to love on Him while you're strong and healthy. Give Him your all while you're strong and in your right mind. Embrace His face and His presence; love on Him until your love goes up to Him as a sweet smelling savor.

When was the last time you kissed the face of God first thing in the morning? You may say that you use to do it before you married, before you had children, before you had the job that you have now. Well try it again. Diamond has never missed a day of kissing me when I get up. Don't allow a dog to show her master more love and appreciation than you show your heavenly father.

Lesson 22

Awareness

One night I was working late at the church doing paperwork with Diamond at my side waiting for me to finish. By the time I'd gotten things wrapped up, it was nearly 2:30 in the morning.

"I have to stop staying at the church so long." I said to her as I tuned out the lights.

I set the alarm, and Diamond and I both went out the door. We have a motion sensor light just outside the door which usually comes on as soon as someone exits the church. To my surprise, the light did not come on because the main switch had been turned off. Without the illumination of the light, it was nearly impossible to see the lock on the door. I felt around, fumbling for the key slot on the lock, secured the building, then turned to go to my car. It was then that Diamond started to growl. I strained in the dark trying to see what had alerted her, but I could make nothing out. It was just too dark. Just as I was ready to get in the car, Diamond began to bark loud and continuously. Heeding her warning, I looking around again, and this time, I saw the silhouette of a man coming towards me but Diamond would not let him get close.

"Hello; can I help you get your things?" he asked.

It was 2:30 in the morning, I thought. "I'm okay, thanks." I responded. "Have a nice night."

With Diamond still on guard, the man turned and walked away. Of course Diamond and I quickly got into the car and went on home. I thank God for her alertness, and His protection, and rewarded Diamond with a kiss and then a treat when we got home.

Diamond . . . A Girl's Best Friend

Even when Diamond eats her food she is constantly aware of her environment and surroundings. While she is eating she continues to look up whenever she hears something move. She is always watching, very attentive of what's going on around her. There have been times that I've walked her outside and she has smelled something underground and began to dig trying to get it to come out. I will always stop her from digging if I notice, however one day I was talking to one of the neighbors and I did not realize she was digging. When I looked Diamond had not only found the animal that was underground but she had it in her mouth! It was unable to hide from her or take her by surprise.

God promises us that He will take care of us for His own sake. I recall another time when we resided at our previous home. I'd come home alone; Ricky was working a night shift, and my daughters were at a sleep over with friends. Diamond wasn't with me either; she was inside the house waiting for me to arrive. The house sat on a very large plot of land, and the driveway was a good 35 yards from the road. I pulled into the yard then went into the trunk of the car to get a few things and take them in with me. Just before I closed the trunk, I heard someone light a match. I heard the sound so clearly it was as if the person was standing right beside me. When I turned around to look there was a man standing at the end of our driveway in the road smoking a cigarette watching me. I walked into the house just as if I would have if he was not there. Once inside, I peeped from a window, ensuring that I couldn't be seen. The man was still there, standing and looking at the house as if he were trying to decide if he should try anything. I called some family to come sit with me, and also called the Police. Oddly when the police arrived, the man was nowhere to be found.

After everything was all over and I settled down, the next day I thought about the whole thing. I wondered how in the world was I able to hear the man strike a match when he was thirty-five yards or more away from me. I had already thanked and praised God for protecting me but when I thought further about the hand of God at work that night I could not help but shout for joy! He is faithful to His word and to all of His promises.

In the Bible there is a story about King Hezekiah who had fallen deathly ill (II Kings 20:1-5). The prophet Isaiah was sent to him by God to let him know that he would die. When Hezekiah heard the word of the Lord spoken by the prophet Isaiah, he cried bitterly before the Lord and prayed. The prophet had already delivered the word and was on his way into the middle of the court ready to leave, but the Lord spoke again to the prophet telling him:

Turn again, and tell Hezekiah the captain of My people, Thus says the Lord, the God of David your father, I have heard your prayer, I have seen your tears; behold, I will heal you: on the third day you shall go up to the house of the Lord. And I will add to your days fifteen years; and I

will deliver you and this city out of the hand of the king of Assyria; and I will defend this city for My own sake, and for My servant David's sake.
– II Kings 20:5-6

I love how God added to Hezekiah's life, and I've always heard people preach about that part of the story yet the part that gets me the most is the alertness of the prophet. Isaiah was so alert and connected to the Lord that after he gave the king the word of the Lord, even while he was leaving he was able to hear the Lord speak again. You know how it is when it's time to go home from work? You have finished for the day and it's as if your mind shuts off. Well, Isaiah had done the work and completed the task, but he was still on the job. Isaiah was in tune to the voice of the Lord, thus able to show Hezekiah that not only does the Lord answer prayers but He will answer them even while you're praying. Psalm 46:10-11 says:

Be still and know that I am God: I will be exalted among the heathen, I will be exalted in the earth. The Lord of hosts is with us; the God of Jacob is our refuge, Selah.

Verse 1 of the same chapter reminds us:

God is our refuge and strength, a very present help in trouble.

Why should we fear anything or anyone in life when we have the almighty God as our refuge?

Conclusion

Diamond has truly been a joy in my life and I love her so much. Who would have thought that her demonstration of love for me, and mine for her would be able to speak so loudly to my spiritual life? From the way she greets me in the morning, to how she leaps for joy when I return home at the end of my day, to how she shows me she knows she can depend on me to take care of her and meet her needs, has truly shown me again how God so dearly loves each and every one of us and how we should love on Him.

My prayer is that you can take something from my wonderful experiences and lessons learned taught to me by God through one of his precious creations . . . a beautiful Diamond, and apply them to your own spiritual life.

Rose M. Jarvis is the Founder of "NYV" Nana's Youth Vision, a non-profit organization that embraces the development of children in the Gloucester, VA communities. She desires to transform lives of all nationalities, helping those that are thirsty for God to live life in the spirit of excellence, bringing glory to God.

Rose graduated from Greenport High School in New York, completed studies with Rhema Bible College, Alpha & Omega College of Real Estate, Boyce Bible College and The Institute of Biblical Studies with Liberty University. She has received Summa Cum Laude honors from Andersonville Theology and is continuing her Biblical Studies with Andersonville Theology pursuing her Ph.D. in Theology. In 2007 she received a Female Preacher award with honors. During 2009 Rose received

Diamond . . . A Girl's Best Friend

the Stover Volunteerism Service Award and the Electrical Sector Community Service Award from Eaton Corporation.

She is the daughter of the late James & Shirley Cosby Carpenter of Long Island, New York and is married to Richard Leon Jarvis. She and Richard are the parents of two beautiful daughters, LaToya Sharice & Felicia Rochelle Jarvis, grandparents to Daveon and Emani, and the proud owners of a wonderful Rat Terrier-Pitt Bull, Diamond.